As one of the world's longest established
                                    nds,
                                    avel.

                                    our
                                    rets
                                    orld,
                                    h of
                                    vel.

**Rely on Thomas Cook as your
travelling companion on your next trip
and benefit from our unique heritage.**

Thomas Cook **pocket** guides

HALKIDIKI

Written and updated by Robin Gauldie
Original photography by www.sargasso-travelimages.com

Published by Thomas Cook Publishing
A division of Thomas Cook Tour Operations Limited
Company registration no. 3772199 England
The Thomas Cook Business Park, Unit 9, Coningsby Road,
Peterborough PE3 8SB, United Kingdom
Email: books@thomascook.com, Tel: +44 (0) 1733 416477
www.thomascookpublishing.com

Produced by Cambridge Publishing Management Limited
Burr Elm Court, Main Street, Caldecote CB23 7NU
www.cambridgepm.co.uk

ISBN: 978-1-84848-385-9

Series Editor: Karen Beaulah
Production/DTP: Steven Collins

Printed and bound in Spain by GraphyCems

Cover photography © Streetlife/Alamy

CONTENTS

INTRODUCTION.........................5
Getting to know Halkidiki............8
The best of Halkidiki...................10
Symbols key 12

RESORTS....................................13
Nea Moudania.............................15
Kallithea.......................................20
Kriopigi...24
Hanioti..26
Pefkohori......................................34
Nea Skioni....................................40
Sani...43
Vourvourou 51
Sarti..54
Porto Koufo 56
Neos Marmaras &
    Porto Carras............................58
Ouranoupolis 63

EXCURSIONS 71
Thessaloniki 73
Mount Athos 79
Naoussa & Vergina......................83
Mount Olympus & Dion.............86
Skiathos & Skopelos 89

LIFESTYLE 93
Food & drink 94
Menu decoder 98
Shopping 100
Children 102
Sports & activities 104
Festivals & events 106

PRACTICAL INFORMATION...109
Accommodation 110
Preparing to go 112
During your stay 116

INDEX 125

MAPS
Halkidiki 6
Kassandra Peninsula....................14
Sani 42
Sithonia Peninsula 52
Mount Athos Peninsula...............62
Thessaloniki 72
Naoussa & Vergina......................82

WHAT'S IN YOUR GUIDEBOOK?

Independent authors Impartial, up-to-date information from our travel experts who meticulously source local knowledge.

Experience Thomas Cook's 165 years in the travel industry and guidebook publishing enriches every word with expertise you can trust.

Travel know-how Thomas Cook has thousands of staff working around the globe, all living and breathing travel.

Editors Travel-publishing professionals, pulling everything together to craft a perfect blend of words, pictures, maps and design.

You, the traveller We deliver a practical, no-nonsense approach to information, geared to how you really use it.

ABOUT THE AUTHOR

Robin Gauldie first visited Greece in 1973 and has returned every year since then. He is the author of several guidebooks, including the *Travellers Guide to Mainland Greece* and *Travellers Guide to the Greek Islands* (both published by Thomas Cook).

● *The unspoilt beach of Karidi, near Vourvourou*

INTRODUCTION
Getting to know Halkidiki

Getting to know Halkidiki

Almost untouched by tourism until the 1980s, Halkidiki has become the most popular holiday region in northern Greece. It has a wide choice of excellent beaches: some are lined with loungers and umbrellas in bustling, purpose-built resorts that offer all kinds of watersports; others are long empty stretches that are perfect for beachcombing. For those who can tear themselves away from Halkidiki's sands for a day or more, Thessaloniki is not far away, with an urban appeal that perfectly complements the laid-back charm of the Halkidiki beaches, and some of Greece's most fascinating (and least visited) ancient sites are accessible with a hired car or on an escorted tour.

WHERE IS HALKIDIKI?

Halkidiki juts out from the north shore of the Aegean Sea, south of Greece's border with Bulgaria and less than 64 km (40 miles) from Thessaloniki, Greece's second-largest city, and its international airport. On the map, it resembles a three-fingered hand, with its fingers outspread and pointing south into the Aegean. The palm of this hand is a rural region of wooded hills and rolling farmland covered with olive groves, wheat fields and vineyards, and dotted with prosperous small market towns. To the north, steep mountain ranges rising to more than 1,200 m (4,000 ft) separate the region from the rest of northern Greece.

THE REAL HALKIDIKI

For many visitors, Kassandra, the westernmost of Halkidiki's three peninsulas, is the most appealing, with some of the best sandy beaches in Greece stretching for miles along its coastline, and steep hills thickly covered with pine forest forming a spectacular backdrop.

Most of Kassandra's best beaches are on its east coast, where there's a near-continuous chain of small resorts between Nea Potidea and Hanioti, with long stretches of white sand and small bays of dazzlingly clear blue water. Kassandra's west coast is rockier, with a scattering of sleepy fishing villages and a handful of very upmarket purpose-built resort hotels.

Sithonia, the middle 'finger' of Halkidiki, is less developed for tourism but no less appealing, with lots of empty small beaches to be discovered by more adventurous visitors. More mountainous than Kassandra, its hinterland is dominated by the rugged 811-m (2,660-ft) massif of Mount Itamos and inland the peninsula is almost completely uninhabited.

From Sithonia's east coast, the third 'finger' of Halkidiki looms large. This is Mount Athos, Greece's 'Holy Mountain' – a unique, self-governing region, studded with spectacular ancient Orthodox monasteries, ruled by monks, and off-limits not just to any visitor without a special permit, but to all women and even to female animals.

● *The irresistible lure of Ekies Hotel beach, Vourvourou*

THE BEST OF HALKIDIKI

Almost everyone who comes to Halkidiki has been drawn by the allure of its beaches, but Greece's second city, Thessaloniki, and some of Greece's most absorbing (and least visited) ancient sites make perfect cultural excursions for those who need some time away from the sand.

TOP 10 ATTRACTIONS

- **Hanioti**, Kassandra's largest resort, has lots of watersports and a beach lined with bustling bars and cafés (see pages 26–33).

- **Pefkohori** has a bustling beach esplanade shaded by tall pine trees; this resort also has vast, deserted stretches of sandy beach just a short walk south of town (see pages 34–9).

- **Vourvourou**, Sithonia's most pleasant resort, has a long curve of yellow sand around a mirror-calm, sheltered bay of warm shallow water (see pages 51 & 53).

- **Ouranoupolis** has excellent beaches either side of the town and an archipelago of tiny islands offshore (see pages 63–70).

- **Sail around Mount Athos** on a day cruise from Sithonia or Ouranoupolis (see pages 51 & 65).

- **Thessaloniki Archaeological Museum** houses extraordinary gold and ivory treasures discovered in the tombs of Alexander's ancestors (see page 76).

- **Museum of Byzantine Culture**, Thessaloniki, displays the glowing colours of centuries-old icons, painted in the heyday of the great Byzantine Empire (see page 76).

- **Market shopping** in Thessaloniki's Modiano and Vlali markets is a feast for the eye, with great piles of fruit and vegetables, weird fish and shellfish, and dozens of different kinds of olives (see pages 100 & 101).

- **A night out in Ladadika**. Thessaloniki's rejuvenated bar and restaurant district lies behind the harbour (see pages 77–8).

- **Head for the hinterland** to visit the Royal Tombs at Vergina, Alexander's birthplace at Pella, or the remains of the ancient city of Dion below Mount Olympus (see pages 83, 84–5 & 86).

⏷ *Panteleimonos Monastery on Mount Athos*

SYMBOLS KEY
The following symbols are used throughout this book:

ⓐ address ⓣ telephone ⓦ website address ⓔ email
ⓛ opening times ⓘ important

The following symbols are used on the maps:

𝑖	information office	○	city
✉	post office	○	large town
▣	shopping	○	small town
✈	airport	■	point of interest
✚	hospital	═	motorway
⛨	police station	—	main road
🚌	bus station	—	minor road
🚆	railway station	—	railway
✝	church	- - -	ferry

❶ numbers denote featured cafés, restaurants & evening venues

RESTAURANT CATEGORIES
The symbol after the name of each restaurant listed in this guide indicates the price of a typical three-course meal without drinks for one person.
£ under €20 ££ €20–€40 £££ over €40

▶ *A traditional village near Porto Carras*

 RESORTS
Places under the sun

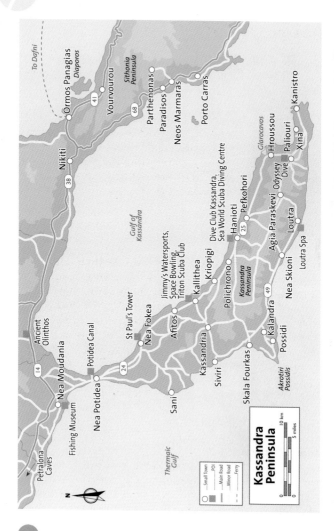

Nea Moudania

Nea Moudania is easily bypassed on the way to Kassandra's more popular resort beaches, but for a taste of real Greek life it is well worth making a trip to this workaday fishing port and market town.

A sizeable fleet of fishing boats sets sail every day from Nea Moudania's harbour, bringing back a haul destined for the dining tables of the holiday hotels of Halkidiki and the fish restaurants of Thessaloniki and Athens. Inland from the harbour and its parade of palm trees, Nea Moudania is a mostly modern community, laid out on a grid pattern, and has all the practical facilities and services that are in short supply in most of the resort areas – including banks and ATMs, pharmacies, travel agencies and supermarkets.

BEACHES

Nea Moudania has its own beach, with loungers, umbrellas, cafés and watersports equipment, such as pedalos and windsurfing boards, for hire. It is located just west of the harbour. There is an even better beach on the west side of Nea Potidea, the small suburb some 6 km (4 miles) south of the centre of Nea Moudania. Nea Potidea straddles the narrow isthmus at the head of the Kassandra Peninsula, and the beach is on the east side of the village. It has hundreds of sunloungers and umbrellas, and at weekends and during the local summer holidays in July and August, when city dwellers from Thessaloniki descend on the Halkidiki beaches in their thousands, it can be very lively indeed.

THINGS TO SEE & DO

Ancient Olinthos

It requires some imagination to visualise this once-great city of ancient times, as all that remains are its foundations, laid out on a hilltop above the main coast road. However, the views from the top of the hill, looking over a patchwork of fields and olive groves to the mountains in one

◆ *Boats cruising down Potidea Canal*

direction, and out to sea in the other, are well worth the walk. What's more, children will enjoy spotting wandering wild tortoises and big green lizards on the way.

The first city here was destroyed by the invading Persians in 479 BC, but was rebuilt to become the capital of a miniature empire of 32 Greek cities and was the most important settlement in Halkidiki until it was sacked by Philip II, King of Macedonia, in 348 BC. Archaeologists began to explore the site in 1928, and since the 1990s further work has been carried out by the Greek government.

ⓐ 8 km (5 miles) east of Nea Moudania, on the north side of the coastal highway, signposted ☎ 23108 01429 🕐 08.30–15.00 Tues–Sun (Mar–Oct)

Fishing Museum

This small museum is dedicated to the history of fishing in Greek waters over the centuries, with a collection that includes ancient anchors, tridents and fish-spears, nets and fish-traps, an early helmet-diver's suit, photos and videos of sea creatures, and a remarkable collection of sea shells.

ⓐ Vithynias 2, Nea Moudania ☎ 23730 26166 🕐 09.00–13.00, 17.00–20.00 Tues–Sun (Mar–Sept)

Petralona Caves

Peculiar limestone formations adorn this cavern, discovered in 1959, but its main claim to fame is as the last resting place of the earliest human European. In 1960, the fossilised skull of a man, dating from around 700,000 years ago, was discovered here, and palaeontologists have also found the fossil bones of long-extinct lions, hyenas, bears, elephants, rhinoceros and bison. There are guided tours in English.

ⓐ 16 km (10 miles) northwest of Nea Moudania, off the main Thessaloniki highway, signposted 🕐 09.00–1 hour before sunset daily

Potidea Canal

This remarkable work of ancient engineering, dating from around the 5th century BC, cuts across the isthmus of the Kassandra Peninsula between Nea Moudania and Nea Potidea. It provides a handy shortcut for yachts, leisure cruisers and fishing boats between the Thermaic Gulf to the west, and the Gulf of Kassandra. Remnants of the medieval city walls, built of massive blocks of stone, can be seen in places on the southern bank of the canal.

ⓐ Potidea, 6 km (4 miles) south of Nea Moudania centre ⓛ 24 hours

St Paul's Tower

Above the small harbour at Nea Fokea, a square 25-m (82-ft) stone tower stands on a headland from which there are great views eastward to Sithonia. Local legend says that St Paul slept here. In fact, the tower is one of the few remaining Byzantine relics in the area dating from a later era, when Greece was already a Christian country.

ⓐ Nea Fokea village, signposted, 16 km (10 miles) southeast of Nea Moudania ⓘ Not open to visitors; can only be viewed from outside

TAKING A BREAK

The centre of Nea Moudania is not well supplied with outstanding bars and restaurants catering for tourists. A better bet is to head south to Nea Potidea, where several café-bars and tavernas cluster along the busy beach near the east end of the canal.

Ta Kastra ££ Excellent fish taverna with indoor and outdoor tables next to the canal, close to the harbour. ⓐ Nea Potidea ⓣ 23730 41411 ⓦ www.kastra.eu ⓛ 12.00–15.00, 19.00–24.00 daily

Taverna Olinthos ££ Unfussy, traditional Greek food, conveniently close to the entrance to Ancient Olinthos (follow the signs from the car park along a short dirt road). ⓐ Ancient Olinthos ⓣ 23730 91666 ⓛ 11.00–15.00 daily

⬤ St Paul's Tower, Nea Fokea

Kallithea

Kallithea means 'beautiful view' – and this resort midway down the east coast of Kassandra lives up to its name. Looking out to sea, the whole of the wide blue Gulf of Kassandra is spread out in front of you, with the mountainous outline of the Sithonia Peninsula to the east. Kallithea is very much a purpose-built resort catering to most tastes. It has a good choice of activities, nightlife and places to eat, along with a number of large modern resort hotels and smaller places to stay. The main section of the resort is laid out on a grid plan, either side of a pedestrianised shopping street, inland from the beach and separated from it by the main east coast highway. Meanwhile, Kallithea's louder and noisier nightlife occupies a designated 'club area' two blocks south of the centre of the resort, west of the main road.

BEACHES

One long, sandy beach stretches the full length of the resort, and is lined almost solidly from one end to the other with sunloungers and parasols. Two small marinas – one at the north end of the beach, the other midway along it – offer watersports and moorings for yachts and motor cruisers. The southern end of the beach is the liveliest section, with a string of beach bars pumping out loud music day and night. However, those wanting a more peaceful space to stretch out will find it by walking a little further south, where the beach is narrower and less busy.

NEW ARRIVALS
To visitors who are familiar with the old villages of the Greek islands, most Halkidiki communities look oddly modern. This isn't surprising: there were very few communities in Kassandra and Sithonia until the early 1920s, when Greek refugees settled here after being expelled from Turkey.

◢ The long beach at Kallithea

THINGS TO SEE & DO

Jimmy's Watersports

Jimmy's rents pedalos, motorboats and canoes, and offers watersports including parascending, waterskiing, jet-skiing, and banana boat and sea biscuit rides. For those less inclined to action, Jimmy's also hires out sunloungers under rows of straw umbrellas.

ⓐ North Marina, Kallithea beach ☏ 69779 16481 🕓 09.00–sunset daily

Space Bowling

This flash, modern games centre has six bowling lanes, plus billiards, table tennis and a range of computer games for adults and children, as well as an open-air garden bar.

ⓐ Club area, main road, Kallithea ☏ 23740 24343 🕓 11.00–24.00 daily

Triton Scuba Club

Triton offers snorkelling and scuba diving, and the clear, calm waters of the Aegean Sea are a perfect place to start. Triton can arrange diving trips – including wreck dives and night dives – as well as learn-to-dive courses for all ages from 8 years upwards.

ⓐ Diving base, Kallithea ☏ 69447 77575 ⓦ www.tritonscuba.gr
🕓 09.00–20.00 daily

TAKING A BREAK

Kallithea has plenty of restaurants and cafés, with a preponderance of fast-food places catering to tourist tastes and serving up pasta, pizzas, burgers and fish and chips, as well as *souvlaki* (see 'Food & drink', page 94) and other Greek grilled food. Few can be singled out for acclaim (and many change their name, owner and menu from one summer season to the next). Honourable exceptions include the following:

Mystic Pizza and Pasta £ Friendly, cheerful Italian-style restaurant with a menu that is predictable from its name. Good value for money for an evening a deux or a family night out. ⓐ Main road, Kallithea ⓣ 23740 21095 ⓛ 12.00–23.00 daily

Aitrion ££ This is one of the prettier eating places in Kallithea, with old-fashioned blue-painted chairs and tables under palm trees and a traditional Greek menu. ⓐ Kallithea main road, at the second entrance to the central shopping walk area ⓣ 23740 22710 ⓛ 12.00–23.00 daily

Café Mpelki ££ Choose this café-bar-restaurant for its legendary view out to sea from a terrace shaded by trees and white canvas umbrellas. ⓐ Corner of Kallithea main road and the last street to the beach ⓣ 23740 23150 ⓛ 11.00–24.00 daily

Perfetto ££ A long-established local favourite, with an Italian–Greek menu and a good choice of pizzas made in its wood-fired oven. ⓐ Corner of 25 Martiou and Kapetan Xapsa ⓣ 23740 23405 ⓛ 12.00–24.00 daily

⬥ Kallithea is a busy, purpose-built resort

Kriopigi

Kriopigi means 'cold stream' – a reminder of the torrents that flow to the sea from Kassandra's hilly interior during the winter months but that dry to a trickle by the beginning of summer. Kriopigi is indeed one of the region's cooler, more laid-back spots, with just 12 or so medium-sized resort hotels plus a good choice of smaller guesthouses and apartment complexes. Kriopigi offers a little more space and a bit less noisy excitement than neighbouring resorts such as Kallithea and Hanioti. Getting to the beach can be a bit of a hike as Kriopigi stands atop quite steep slopes above the sea, making this resort less than perfect for those with babies or toddlers, or with mobility difficulties. Inland, the original village has more character than most Halkidiki resorts, with streets lined with old red-roofed houses, while most of the newer cafés, bars, tavernas and accommodation are located between the main road and the beach.

BEACHES

Kriopigi's beach runs the full length of the resort. There is plenty of sand, but it is admittedly narrower and less spectacular than the breathtaking strands of the resorts to the north and south. To compensate, it is also a good deal less crowded than its neighbours.

THINGS TO SEE & DO

Kriopigi has the usual selection of watersports outfits offering canoes, pedalos, waterskiing and parascending. The names and faces change

BLUE FLAG BEACHES

Halkidiki has more 'Blue Flag' beaches than any other region of Greece, with more than 40 of its beaches receiving Blue Flag certification for water purity and cleanliness above the tideline each year.

from summer to summer, so no listings are given here. For a wider range of activities and excursions, Hanioti (see pages 26–9) is just 10 km (6¹/₂ miles) southeast of Kriopigi.

TAKING A BREAK

Plateia tis Anthoulas £ This traditional taverna serving grills and oven-cooked dishes such as *moussaka* (see 'Local food', page 96) is a local favourite. ⓐ Plateia tis Kriopigis (main square), Kriopigi, above and to the right of the main road ⓣ 23740 53001 ⓛ 19.00–24.00 Mon–Thur, 12.00–15.00, 19.00–24.00 Fri–Sun

⬯ A steep hill runs down to Kriopigi's narrow beach

Hanioti

Hanioti is the biggest and liveliest of the resorts on the east coast of Kassandra. It has grown up around a central square lined with tavernas, bars and shops, and is very much a town that lives off tourism, with all the shops, restaurants, bars, guesthouses and hotels you could possibly desire. For all that, its tree-lined streets are surprisingly peaceful, with very little traffic (cars are banned from the village centre after dark). What's more, there's plenty of shade during the day from the pines, palms and plane trees along the roadsides, plus pretty splashes of purple bougainvillea and crimson geraniums in pots and window boxes. Midway along the seafront, immediately inland from the beach, is a leafy green park beside which stands an attractive old white-painted church. Hanioti's lively, bar-based after-dark scene spreads out around the central square and along the beach. Restaurants range from Indian, Mexican and Italian to Russian and German.

BEACHES

Hanioti's beach is one of the best in the Kassandra region – and one of the most popular. A long, broad strip of clean white sand, living up to its 'Blue Flag' label, stretches all the way along the waterfront. Throughout the summer season, it is studded with brightly coloured umbrellas, and there are several lively beach bars that pump out music throughout the day. A long esplanade lined with trees runs all the way along the beach. Hanioti virtually merges with the smaller resort of Polichrono, only 5 km (3 miles) to the northwest, along a continuous strip of sea and sand.

THINGS TO SEE & DO

Diving

The waters around the Kassandra and Sithonia peninsulas offer some of the best diving in Greece for novice and experienced divers. Visibility is excellent and there is lots to see, from the wreck of the MV *Mitilini* just

◗ *Halkidiki's trademark white sand and clear sea in Hanioti*

10 minutes offshore to caves and reefs where divers can see big groupers, moray eel, octopus and sometimes even dolphins. Dive centres to try are:

Dive Club Kassandra Snorkel and scuba trips, 'discover scuba' dives, PADI training courses and scuba equipment rental.

ⓐ Centre of Hanioti, near the square ⓣ 69765 19041

ⓦ www.divecenter-kassandra.de.vu ⓛ 08.00–12.00, 16.00–20.00 daily

Sea World Scuba Diving Centre PADI training courses for people aged 10 and over as well as dive cruises for those who already have their diver's qualification.

ⓐ Hanioti ⓣ 23740 53358 ⓦ www.seaworld.gr ⓛ 08.00–12.00, 16.00–20.00 daily

Sunset cruises

Sunset cruises along the coast can be booked at all the main hotels in Hanioti and at the watersports centre at the north end of the beach. These cruises are billed as 'romantic', but the rock music and free-flowing beer turn them into a regular floating party.

Thessaloniki sightseeing trips

Hanioti Tours runs small-group minibus tours to the sights of Thessaloniki and further afield, as well as tailor-made private sightseeing trips.

ⓐ Plateia Haniotis (central square) ⓣ 23740 53320 ⓦ www.haniotitours.gr

ⓛ 09.00–12.00, 15.00–20.00 daily

Watersports

Alexandros Watersports offers parascending, pedalos and canoes. Neither of these has telephone or website – just turn up and go.

ⓛ 09.00–sunset daily

Watersports Center offers canoes, pedalos, banana boat and sea ring rides, jet-skis and waterskis from the northern end of the beach (just past the north end of the park and in front of the Grand Otel).

ⓐ At the south end of the beach (in front of the Molos Beach Bar).

⬥ *Pedalos are one of the many water activities on offer*

TAKING A BREAK

Drami's £ Provides an introduction to some of the things Greece does best: sticky pastries such as *baklava*, croissants, doughnuts, cakes and the best *bougatsa* (Greek custard pie) in town. ⓐ Main road, Hanioti ⓣ 23740 52907 ⓛ 11.00–23.00 daily

Roma Pizza £ This restaurant is part of Greece's biggest pizza chain and serves a big choice of pizzas in all sizes to eat in or take away. ⓐ Plateia Haniotis (central square) ⓣ 23740 52122 ⓦ www.romapizza.gr ⓛ 12.00–24.00 daily

Zorbas Tavern ££ Hanioti's oldest and most authentic Greek restaurant has been in business since 1978. It serves steaks and other grills, fresh seafood, salads and pasta dishes. ⓐ Two blocks south of Plateia Haniotis (central square) ⓣ 23740 52127 ⓦ www.zorbas-tavern.gr ⓛ 12.00–15.00, 19.00–24.00 daily

WHAT'S IN A NAME?

Halkidiki forms part of the Greek region of Macedonia, named after the ancient realm of Alexander the Great and Philip, his son. The right to use the name is a bone of contention between Greece and its northern neighbour, the Former Yugoslav Republic of Macedonia, which is generally known in Greece by the acronym FYROM. Greece refuses to concede FYROM the right to call itself Macedonia and, despite meetings in late 2010 between Greek prime minister George Papandreou and his FYROM opposite number Nikola Gruevski, the issue seems as far as ever from being resolved, with neither side willing to back down and Greece continuing to veto Macedonia's accession to the European Union until it gives way.

⬥ The picturesque church of Agios Ioannis in Hanioti

◐ *An attractive park lies just inland from Hanioti's beach*

Zytheion Beer House ££ Zytheion boasts that it sells more brands of beer (over 100) than any other restaurant in Hanioti and also serves a range of Greek, Russian and German dishes including pasta and German sausage. ⓐ Plateia Haniotis (central square) ⓣ 23740 51900 ⓛ 11.00–02.00 daily

AFTER DARK

Billy's Bar £ This bar offers crowd-pleasing entertainment ranging from snooker and arcade games to karaoke on Saturday nights. It also has Internet access as well as a range of chilled beers and cocktails. ⓐ Plateia Haniotis (central square) ⓣ 23740 51445 ⓛ 09.00–02.00 daily

Molos Beach Bar £ At the south end of Hanioti beach, Molos is an excellent place to chill during the day or after dark. ⓐ Hanioti beach ⓣ 23740 52133 ⓛ 11.00–02.00 (June–Sept)

Bahalo Spiaggia ££ Right in front of the park, midway along the beach, Bahalo rocks almost all day and virtually all night. During the day it serves beer and other cold drinks and snacks; after sunset it mutates into a loud and lively music bar. ⓐ Hanioti beach ⓣ 23740 62111 ⓛ 11.00–02.00 (June–Sept)

SunShine ££ This lively bar with its comfy leather sofas is one of the best in Hanioti. It is open during the day but really takes off after dark, with a list of surprising and potent cocktails. ⓐ Plateia Haniotis (central square) ⓛ 11.00–02.00 (June–Sept)

Waikiki Summer Bar ££ This popular nightspot offers two cocktails for the price of one from 18.00 to 20.00, with predictable results. It also offers sports TV. ⓐ Hanioti beach ⓛ 12.00–02.00 (June–Sept)

Pefkohori

An enormous swathe of beach stretches as far as the eye can see on either side of Pefkohori. The village's name means 'pine village' (it was renamed in 1964) and it is very apt: an avenue of tall pines shades the beach, and in high summer the cicadas that live in the trees sing so loudly they can be heard over the throbbing beats issuing from the village's string of beach bars.

Like most Kassandra resort villages, Pefkohori has a modern section between the main road and the sea, where most of the restaurants, bars, hotels and other holiday essentials can be found. A little way inland is the older, calmer part of the village, with red-tiled homes and pretty gardens filled with flowers in the older streets around the church square, just south of the main road. A small jetty, from which excursion boats sail to Mount Athos and around the coast, juts into the sea from the north end of the beach.

⬤ *Fishing boats are a common sight in Glarocavos, south of Pefkohori*

BEACHES

Pefkohori is strategically sited roughly midway along the longest continuous stretch of beach on the Kassandra Peninsula – a 14-km (9-mile) swathe of white sand broken by occasional pebbly patches. Most people prefer to wander no further than the serried ranks of loungers and umbrellas that stretch along the village seafront, along which runs a wooden boardwalk connecting a string of beach bars and restaurants. But those who prefer a little more solitude need only head a short distance south to find near-deserted stretches. Around 8 km (5 miles) southeast of the village, at Glarocavos, is a large, blue-water lagoon where a flotilla of fishing boats and yachts lies at anchor. There is a small, basic and nameless summer cantina (snack bar) beneath the pine trees between the beach and lagoon. There is a smaller and even more remote beach at Xina, close to the southern tip of Kassandra and around 16 km (10 miles) southeast of Pefkohori. However, there are no beach facilities here, so visitors need a rented car to bring all their own comforts and supplies (including plenty of water).

THINGS TO SEE & DO

Agia Paraskevi
High above the coast and set among pinewoods, this old-fashioned village seems a world away from the beaches and bars of Pefkohori. Unlike their coastal cousins, people here still make their living from their olive groves, vineyards and beehives, and the village square has a cluster of sleepy traditional cafés where you can sip an *ouzo* or a tiny cup of Greek coffee.
ⓐ 8 km (5 miles) south of Pefkohori, 6 km (4 miles) west of Paliouri, on the main road

Diving
Odyssey Dive offers the full range of PADI courses and facilities and a big choice of dives all around the waters of Halkidiki.
ⓐ Giannikos Hotel, Paliouri ⓣ 06976 762282 ⓦ www.odysseydive.com

◯ *A deserted stretch of sand in Pefkohori*

Kanistro

The tiny settlement at Kanistro is no more than a handful of fishermen's cottages around a miniature harbour, overlooked by a tiny white-painted chapel on a headland. But its position at the very tip of the Kassandra Peninsula means that it boasts grand views to the south, east and west. It makes a good destination for a morning's exploring in a rented car, and is worth a visit just for that 'world's end' feeling. The beach doesn't match up to the bigger and busier strands elsewhere on Kassandra, but it's adequate for a quick dip before driving on or homeward – and it's certainly uncrowded.

🅐 20 km (13 miles) southeast of Pefkohori, signposted on the left just before Paliouri on the main road

Loutra Spa

This modern spa, which attracts a mainly Greek clientele, stands on a hillside above the sea. Loutra's natural thermal springs have been renowned for their healing properties since Roman times, and the naturally heated pools are now complemented by an array of modern therapeutic treatments and facilities, including sauna and hammam, hydromassage and specialist treatments for skin complaints, rheumatism, arthritis, asthma and other ailments. The stink-bomb smell of sulphur hangs over the entire hillside, a natural by-product of the subterranean waters that bubble to the surface from deep in the rock below.

🅐 Loutra, 20km (13 miles) southwest of Pefkohori, on the main road
🅣 23740 71358 🆆 www.loutrahalkidikis.gr 🅛 08.00–19.30 Mon–Sat, 08.00–15.30 Sun

TAKING A BREAK

Roma Pizza £ A cheap and cheerful option whether you want a sit-down meal or a pizza with all the trimmings to take back to your apartment.
🅐 Main road, Pefkohori 🅣 80111 69000 🆆 www.romapizza.gr
🅛 12.00–24.00 daily

◉ *The jetty at Pefkohori*

Akti tou Vlachou ££ Classic taverna serving big platters of seafood snacks, excellent fresh fish, salads, grills and oven-cooked dishes. ⓐ Pefkohori beach ① 23740 62428 ② 12.00–16.00, 19.00–23.00 daily

Maxim's ££ This long-established restaurant serves all the standard Greek staples, but the dishes are prepared and served to a higher than average standard and service is friendly. ⓐ Main road, Pefkohori ① 23740 61748 ② 12.00–15.00, 18.00–24.00 daily (Apr–Oct)

Ta Kimata ££ This taverna has a loyal repeat clientele among frequent visitors to Pefkohori. It serves an array of Greek favourites and international dishes. ⓐ Main road, Pefkohori ① 23740 81287 ② 12.00–15.00, 19.00–01.00 daily

AFTER DARK

The Barn £ This long-established Pefkohori nightspot has a decidedly Celtic flavour, with British beers, karaoke nights and a happy hour from 18.00 to 20.00. ⓐ Beach road ① 23740 63162 ② 11.00–02.00 daily

NoNo £££ Pefkohori's premier dance and music club rocks every night, all summer long. Tuesday night is Ladies' Night, Thursday night is Greek night and Saturdays are devoted to R&B. ⓐ On the west side of the main road, around 100 m (110 yds) north of the taxi rank ⓦ www.pefkohorivillage.com ② 21.00–03.00 daily

Nea Skioni

More a genuine fishing and farming village than a fully fledged holiday resort, Nea Skioni is one of the few places on the Kassandra Peninsula where the visitor can sample the real Greece. The village is built around a small harbour, which is home to a flotilla of fishing boats. Indeed, there is a sense that beneath the veneer of tourism this is also a working village with a life of its own. Inland, the villagers own olive groves, vineyards and orchards.

BEACHES

There is a small, busy but well-kept beach with umbrellas, sunloungers and (in high season) lifeguards just south of the harbour. The coast to either side of Nea Skioni is rocky and inhospitable, but there are more beaches, plus a scattering of summer cantinas at Possidi and Skala Fourkas, on either side of the headland of Akrotiri Possidis (Cape Possidi) some 18 km (11 miles) northwest of Nea Skioni, just west of Kalandra, off the main coast road.

THINGS TO SEE & DO

Kanistro, Agia Paraskevi & Loutra
The tip of Kassandra at Kanistro, the old-fashioned hill village of Agia Paraskevi, and the thermal springs at Loutra are as easy to get to from Nea Skioni as from Pefkohori. For details, see pages 35 & 37.

TAKING A BREAK

Vila Stasa ££ Stuffed squid is among the local specialities on the menu at this attractive fish tavern under the pines on the outskirts of Loutra. Well worth making the short journey for a special meal. ⓐ Loutra, 5 km (3 miles) southeast of Nea Skioni ⓘ 23740 71227 ⓛ 12.00–15.00, 19.00–24.00 daily

A day's cruise can be the highlight of a holiday

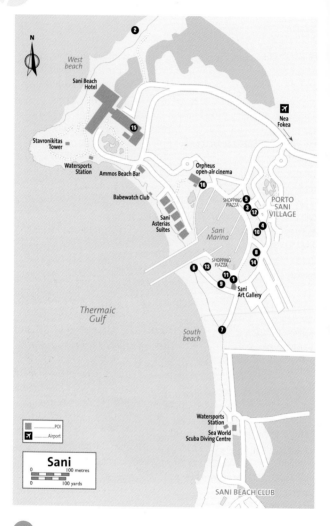

Sani

Opened in 1971 as the Sani Beach Club, Sani Resort has grown into a huge luxury resort set on the west coast of the Kassandra Peninsula on a 400-ha (1,000-acre) ecological reserve. It comprises four luxury hotels (two rated 5 star and two rated 4 star), built around Sani Marina, a private harbour filled with gleaming white yachts and leisure cruisers surrounded by smart boutiques and an array of fine restaurants, tavernas, café-bars and traditional *ouzeries*.

Accommodation ranges from individual villas set on a private white sand beach to family houses, an all-suite spa hotel and the core of the resort, the 450-room Sani Beach Hotel. Sani also has a big choice of sports and watersports facilities, and excellent facilities for families with children, including at least nine swimming pools.

ⓘ The resort and all its restaurants, bars and leisure facilities close from late October to Easter

BEACHES

Sani's white, sandy beaches extend both north and south of a rocky headland crowned by the ancient stones of a Byzantine fortress, the Stavronikitas Tower. Each hotel within the complex has its own stretch of beach, lined with white canvas umbrellas and beach loungers, and each with its own beach bar.

The Sani Beach Hotel faces northwest over the stretch of beach north of the headland. On the other side, facing southwest, is the resort's most exclusive strip of private beach, between the headland and the marina and overlooked by the five-star Sani Asterias Suites. Part of this beach is designated for families with small children.

On the other side of the bay, the Sani Beach Club dominates another lovely white sand beach. However, Sani Resort does not quite manage to entirely monopolise this coast. A cluster of independent summer cantinas and a cheap and cheerful family campsite share the strand between the marina and the Sani Beach Club and provide a valuable budget alternative to its luxury rooms, restaurants and upmarket nightlife.

THINGS TO SEE & DO

Art & culture

The Sani Resort hosts an array of internationally acclaimed performers each summer during the annual **Sani Festival** (mid-July to end of August), which features leading jazz, classical and ethnic musicians from all over the world. At the same time, the **Sani Art Gallery** beside Sani Marina holds a series of fine art exhibitions from July to September.

ⓐ Sani Resort ⓣ 23740 99400 ⓦ www.sani-resort.com

Children & teens

Babewatch Club Beach attendants are available on request to play with and look after small children for up to 30 minutes each day, allowing parents to take a little time off. Available to all guests at Porto Sani Village and Sani Asterias Suites free of charge.

ⓐ Sani Resort ⓣ 23740 99400 ⓦ www.sani-resort.com

Break dancing The Sani Resort runs five-day 'break-dancing camps' for 12–17-year-olds during selected weeks each summer, with professional tuition from the resort's sports and entertainment team.

ⓐ Sani Resort ⓣ 23740 99400 ⓦ www.sani-resort.com

Melissa Mini Club and Crèche Offers a wide and imaginative range of excursions, outdoor sports and indoor activities for children aged 4–16. There is also a crèche for children aged 6 months to 4 years, with activities such as finger-painting, ball games and singalongs.

ⓐ Sani Resort ⓣ 23740 99400 ⓦ www.sani-resort.com

Paintball Park A section of the woodland around Sani is turned into a paintball combat zone for energetic 14–17-year-olds in July and August.

Safety equipment (including goggles and helmets), guns and ammunition are provided.

ⓐ Sani Resort ⓣ 23740 99400 ⓦ www.sani-resort.com

Mountain biking

Bikes for children and adults can be rented at the resort's mountain-bike centre. Guided tours for individuals, groups and families are also available.

ⓐ Sani Resort ⓣ 23740 99400 ⓦ www.sani-resort.com

Orpheus open-air cinema

The Orpheus open-air cinema, next to Sani Marina, shows the latest films in their original language (usually in English, but with some German and Russian offerings too) with Greek subtitles.

ⓐ Sani Resort ⓣ 23740 99400 ⓛ June–Sept

Scuba diving

Sea World Scuba Diving Centre This PADI-certified diving centre offers a full range of learn-to-dive courses and a variety of dive trips for novices and experienced divers.

ⓐ Located next to Sani Beach Club ⓣ 23740 31745 ⓦ www.seaworld.gr

Sunset cruises

Watch the sun set over Mount Olympus far to the west while sipping a chilled cocktail. Cruises leave late afternoon from West beach, north of the Sani Beach Hotel. Reservations are required.

ⓐ Bousoulas Beach Bar, West beach ⓣ 23740 99418 ext 8334
ⓦ www.sani-resort.com

Tennis

Tennis fans are well provided for here. The Sani Beach Hotel's sports complex has six clay courts (two of which are floodlit). Professional coaching is available for individuals, families and groups, and equipment can be hired.

ⓐ Sani Beach Hotel ⓣ 23740 99428 ⓦ www.sani-resort.com
ⓛ 07.00–22.00 daily

⬤ *Each of Sani's hotels has its own stretch of beach*

Watersports

Windsurfing, waterskiing, pedalos, canoes and sailing catamarans are all available from the resort's watersports centre at the south side of the bay, next to the Sani Beach Club, and at West beach next to the Sani Beach Hotel.

ⓐ Sani Resort ❶ 23740 99400 ⓦ www.sani-resort.com

Wildlife & walking

A network of waymarked trails leads through the woodland and meadows of Sani's own nature reserve. The nearby lagoons are a refuge for migrant birds, including mute swans, black-winged stilts, little egrets and even the occasional pelican.

TAKING A BREAK

All the restaurants, bars and cafés at Sani Marina are open to visitors as well as guests staying at the hotels.

Cafés & bars

Art Café ££ ❶ Casual café serving a variety of coffees, teas and tisanes, and freshly squeezed fruit and vegetable juices. ⓐ Sani Marina ❶ 23740 99464 ext 8517 🕒 10.00–22.00 daily

Bousoulas Beach Bar ££ ❷ Serves cocktails, beers, soft drinks, coffee, salads, burgers and snacks on the beach. ⓐ West beach ❶ 23740 99418 🕒 10.00–20.00 daily

Creperie ££ ❸ Casual, family-friendly café-restaurant serving crêpes, snacks, sandwiches and hot and cold drinks. ⓐ Sani Marina ❶ 23740 99562 ext 8552 🕒 09.00–22.00 daily

Patisserie ££ ❹ Pastries, cakes, hot and cold drinks, snacks and sandwiches. Very casual and child-friendly. ⓐ Sani Marina ❶ 23740 99566 ext 8556 🕒 09.00–22.00 daily

◆ *Cool off at Mojito Bar, Sani*

Mojito Bar £££ ❺ Stylish lounge bar serving cocktails, champagne and a range of premium spirits, wine and beers. ⓐ Sani Marina ① 23740 99561 ext 8551 ① 12.00–02.00 daily

Sea You Bar £££ ❻ This is the place to go for sunset cocktails, a glass of champagne, Asian snacks or a cold drink during the day. ⓐ Sani Marina ① 23740 99517 ext 8537 ① 11.00–24.00 daily

Restaurants
Barba Giorgis £ ❼ This cheap and cheerful taverna offers a laid-back, budget alternative to the Sani Marina's posh eateries and serves all the Greek classics from salad to *moussaka*. ⓐ Blue Dream Camping, midway along Sani South beach ① 23740 31249 ⓦ www.campingbluedream.gr ① 09.00–23.00 daily

Alexis Taverna ££ ❽ Traditional-style taverna serving fish and other seafood, grills and salads. ⓐ Sani Marina ① 23740 31176 ① 12.00–15.00, 19.00–24.00 daily

Beef Steki ££ ❾ Child-friendly restaurant serving a variety of burgers and salads. ⓐ Sani Marina ① 23740 99466 ① 12.00–22.00 daily

Macaronissimo ££ ❿ Home-made pasta, meat, fish and modern Italian recipes. ⓐ Sani Marina ① 23740 99567 ext 8557 ① 19.00–24.00 daily ① Reservations required

Tomata ££ ⓫ Award-winning restaurant serving Greek and Mediterranean-fusion dishes in a casual atmosphere. ⓐ Sani Marina ① 23740 99465 ① 19.00–24.00 daily ① Reservations required

Psaroyannos Ouzerie £££ ⓬ Fresh local seafood and other Greek meals and snacks. ⓐ Sani Marina ① 23740 31560 ext 8554 ① 12.00–15.00, 19.00–24.00 daily ① Reservations required

Sea You Up £££ ⓭   This restaurant overlooking the marina and the beach serves an outstanding fusion of Mediterranean and Asian cuisine, especially seafood. ⓐ Sani Marina ⓣ 23740 99517 ext 8537 ⓛ 12.00–15.00, 19.00–24.00 daily ⓘ Reservations required

Vosporos Grill House £££ ⓮   This casual Greek-style grill restaurant is a meat-eater's delight, serving lamb, chicken, pork and steaks. ⓐ Sani Marina ⓣ 23740 31640 ⓛ 12.00–15.00, 19.00–24.00 daily

AFTER DARK

Nautilus Night Club ⓯   This is Sani's main nightspot, playing dance music but aimed at a wealthier and more mature audience than most of Kassandra's clubs. ⓐ Sani Beach Hotel ⓣ 23740 99400 ext 8831 ⓛ 20.00–02.00 daily

Water Bar ⓰   Serves posh after-dinner drinks at Sani's most exclusive bar, with jazz, ethnic and easy-listening music. ⓐ Sani Marina ⓣ 23740 99531 ext 8101 ⓛ 19.00–02.00 daily ⓘ Reservations required

Vourvourou

The tiny, peaceful resort village of Vourvourou sits on the east coast of the Sithonia Peninsula, on a north-facing bay sheltered from the open water of the Gulf of Agion Oros by the uninhabited island of Diaporos. Steep pine-covered slopes rise behind the village, which stretches for around 4 km (2¹/₂ miles) along the bay and has a scattering of small hotels and guesthouses, beachside taverns and mini-markets.

BEACHES

Vourvourou's long beach is a sandy crescent along the south shore of the sheltered bay. The water is shallow (you need to wade out for about 90 m (300 ft) before it is deep enough for swimming), usually very calm and is quickly warmed by the summer sun. East of Vourvourou, and separated from it by a headland of sea-sculpted basalt boulders covered with juniper bushes and wild flowers, is Karidi, a crescent of fine white sand and bright turquoise water.

THINGS TO SEE & DO

Mount Athos is temptingly close. Excursion boats sail every morning in summer from the small harbour at Ormos Panagias, 8 km (5 miles) north of Vourvourou on the main road, on cruises that allow passengers to view some of the mountain's remarkable monasteries and which usually call at the port of Ouranoupolis as well. Motorboats can also be rented at Vourvourou to explore its lagoon and archipelago of uninhabited offshore islets and gorgeous blue bays that can only be reached by boat.

TAKING A BREAK

Ekies ££ Midway along the beach at Vourvourou and also within walking distance of Karidi, this excellent restaurant is part of a delightful, stylish

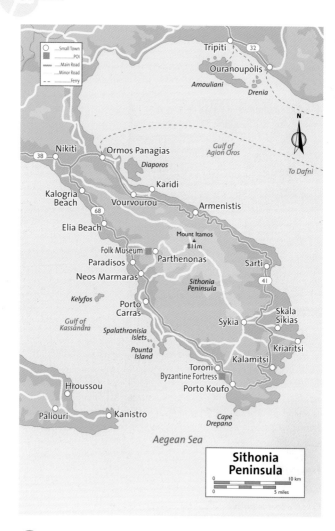

Sithonia
Peninsula

small hotel. The menu is modern Greek, with excellent appetiser plates for a light lunch and an array of more substantial dishes for hungrier diners. ⓐ Vourvourou beach ⓣ 23750 91000 ⓦ www.ekies.gr ⓛ 12.00–24.00 daily (Easter–Sept)

⬤ Rent a boat to explore the blue lagoon near Vourvourou

Sarti

The east coast of Sithonia is rocky and inaccessible for much of its length, and Sarti is the only resort of any size in this part of Halkidiki. It stretches in a spread of small hotels and restaurants along a huge sweep of white sand, facing across to the pinnacle of Mount Athos. There are no large hotels, and Sarti is not for those looking for sophisticated, cosmopolitan accommodation, shopping or nightlife. It attracts more Greek holidaymakers than foreign visitors, and has a lively beach-bar season catering mainly to young Greeks in July and August.

BEACHES

Sarti's huge beach is its main attraction – almost 2 km (1 mile) of clean white sand, facing east. Sunloungers and umbrellas can be rented, and there are several small seasonal beach cantinas where you can buy cold drinks and snacks.

TAKING A BREAK

Alexander the Great £ Pleasant beach restaurant with tables on the sand beneath palm trees and umbrellas. The menu includes most of the Greek favourites: grills, salads and fresh seafood. ❷ South end of Sarti beach ❶ 23740 22991 ❶ 12.00–24.00 daily (June–Sept)

AFTER DARK

Goa ££ At the north end of Sarti's huge beach (where its throbbing beats won't disturb the locals), this beach bar and open-air dance club attracts a lively audience of young Greeks every night, starting with sunset cocktails and rocking until the early hours. ❸ Sarti beach ⓦ www.goa.gr ❶ 12.00–02.00 daily (June–Aug)

○ Sarti's extensive beach offers marvellous lounging opportunities

Porto Koufo

A few yachts and a small fleet of tuna boats add interest to this little fishing village, built around a fine natural harbour on a deep inlet on the west coast of Sithonia, close to Cape Drepano at the southern tip of the peninsula. This is very definitely a spot for those looking to get away from it all; it has no more than a handful of tavernas (serving excellent fresh fish) and some small places to stay.

BEACHES

Porto Koufo's beach is around 1 km (½ mile) south of the village and harbour. A clean but narrow strip of sand and shingle, it has no facilities and does not bear comparison with other beaches on Sithonia and Kassandra.

THINGS TO SEE & DO

A waymarked **walking trail** through the thickly wooded foothills of **Mount Itamos** starts and finishes at the hill village of Sykia, about 10 km (6½ miles) northeast of Porto Koufo. At **Toroni**, about 3 km (2 miles) northwest of Porto Koufo on the coast road, the ruins of a medieval **Byzantine Fortress** stand on a hillock at the end of a wide, sandy bay.

TAKING A BREAK

Psarotaverna o Kapetan Xarsas £ Seafood restaurant overlooking the harbour. ⓐ Porto Koufos harbour ⓣ 23750 51244 ⓛ 12.00–15.00, 19.00–22.00 daily (Easter–Sept); 12.00–15.00, 19.00–22.00 Sat & Sun (Oct–Easter)

Delfini ££ Located on the hillside above the harbour, this fish restaurant is a very pleasant place for a leisurely dinner. ⓐ Porto Koufos ⓣ 23750 51311 ⓛ 12.00–15.00, 19.00–22.00 daily (Easter–Sept); 12.00–15.00, 19.00–22.00 Sat & Sun (Oct–Easter)

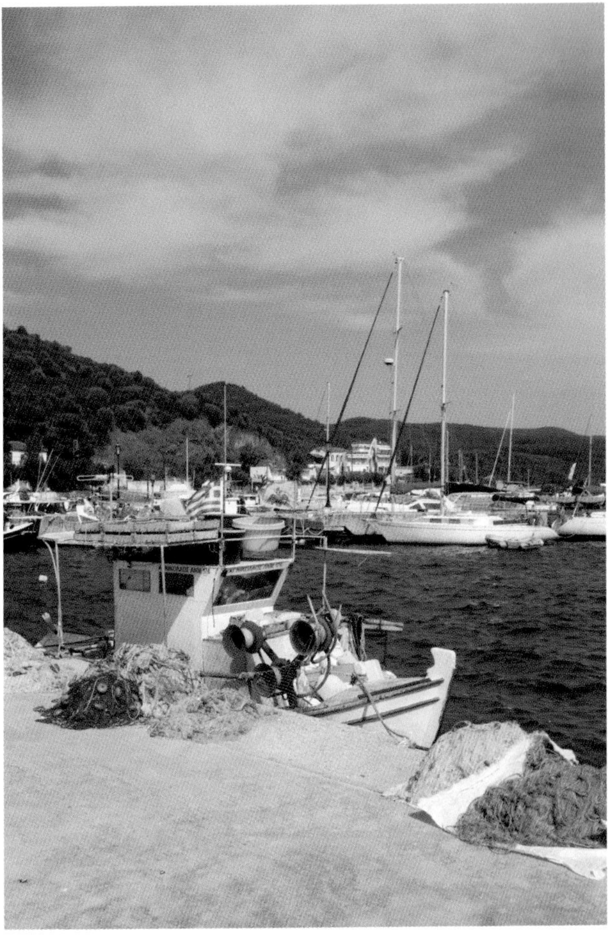

Porto Koufo's fishing harbour

Neos Marmaras & Porto Carras

Neos Marmaras straddles a rocky headland at the north end of a huge sweep of white sand, beneath the wooded slopes of Sithonia's highest mountain, Mount Itamos. Outside tourist season, it is a prosperous fishing and farming community, but from June to September, it is a lively, busy holiday hotspot, with plenty of small hotels and guesthouses, plus numerous restaurants and bars clustered around its small harbour. About 3 km (2 miles) south of the village is the huge Porto Carras resort complex, resembling nothing so much as a fleet of cruise liners located amid its own expanse of golf courses, olive groves, vineyards, sculpted pools and a private marina.

BEACHES

A long sandy beach stretches southwards from Neos Marmaras all the way to Porto Carras. An even better expanse of white sand, with an array of watersports and serried ranks of sunloungers outside a scattering of summer beach bars, can be found at Paradisos, about 3 km (2 miles) north of Neos Marmaras village. Porto Carras has its own semi-private stretch of beach, with all the services and facilities you would expect from a top luxury resort.

THINGS TO SEE & DO

In the hills above Neos Marmaras, the old-fashioned village of Parthenonas makes a pleasant outing. Almost all the village's residents left in the 1970s for new homes in Neos Marmaras. However, the former ghost village is now being restored, with attractive old stone houses being turned into stylish hotels and holiday homes nestling on the picturesque hillside. A small **folk museum** (open irregularly) next to the historic village church explains the history of the region. A network of waymarked **walking trails** leads from Parthenonas around the wooded slopes of Mount Itamos, and for those with the energy to hike to the

811-m (2,660-ft) summit there are fabulous views eastward to Mount Athos and westward to Kassandra.

Excursion boats also sail daily in summer on cruises around the monasteries of Mount Athos. Motorboats can be rented from the harbour for snorkelling and spear-fishing trips to the uninhabited islands of Kelyfos, Pounta and the Spalathronisia islets, about 8 km (5 miles) offshore.

Porto Carras offers a wide range of activities, including golf on three courses, nine tennis courts, scuba diving, mountain biking, horse riding and a full complement of watersports.

⬤ *Sithonia Hotel, in the Porto Carras resort complex*

🔺 *You can eat out, looking over the harbour at Neos Marmaras*

TAKING A BREAK

Kiani Akti ££ Traditional Greek cooking, with a good choice of Greek vegetarian dishes such as stuffed peppers, casseroled green beans and aubergine, plus meat and fish dishes. ② North end of Neos Marmaras beach ① 23750 71290 ① 12.00–15.00, 19.00–22.00 daily

Kimata ££ Excellent fresh local seafood and good salads are served here, beside a harbour full of little fishing boats. ② Neos Marmaras harbour ① 23750 71371 ① 12.00–15.00, 19.00–23.00 daily (Mar–Oct)

Mythos ££ This friendly beach bar at Paradisos serves salads, cold drinks, snacks and light meals all day and into the evening. ② Paradisos beach, Neos Marmaras ① 12.00–22.00 daily

Thessalonikia ££ This friendly, family-run fish restaurant always has a good selection of locally sourced seafood. ② Neos Marmaras harbour ① 23750 71019 ① 12.00–15.00, 19.00–23.00 daily (Easter–Sept)

To Steki tou Meliou ££ About 200 m (650 ft) above the centre of Parthenonas village, this grill restaurant has breathtaking views and a meat-heavy menu featuring lamb, pork, chicken and steaks. ② Parthenonas village, 5 km (3 miles) northeast of Neos Marmaras ① 23750 71686 ① 12.00–15.00, 19.00–23.00 daily (May–Oct)

Xaris £££ Xaris is one of the more expensive restaurants in town but its choice of fresh fish and other seafood, simply prepared, is excellent. ② Main street, Neos Marmaras ① 23750 71465 ① 12.00–15.00, 19.00–23.00 daily (Jan–Sept)

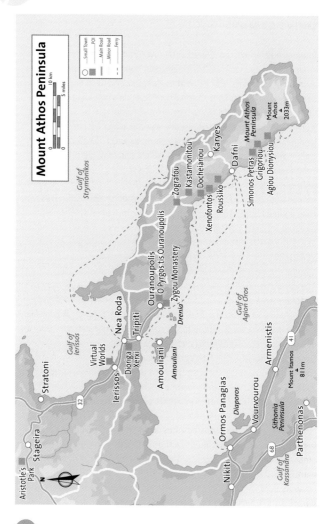

Ouranoupolis

Ouranoupolis is the only resort on Mount Athos, the easternmost of the three Halkidiki peninsulas. It is located just south of the isthmus that connects the peninsula to the rest of Halkidiki, and faces west towards Sithonia. For many visitors – including Orthodox monks and pilgrims – the primary reason for coming here is to travel onward to the isolated monasteries of the 'Holy Mountain'. These are accessible only by sea. A barrier of barbed wire and concrete, reminiscent of the former Berlin Wall, protects them from unwanted visitors, and crossing it is strictly forbidden. But Ouranoupolis is also worth a visit for its excellent and relatively uncrowded sandy beaches. Just offshore lies Drenia, an archipelago of tiny islands, around which is good scuba diving. There are also plenty of places to stay, ranging from campsites on the beach to luxury hotels with private beaches.

BEACHES

A series of crescent bays with lovely white sand beaches, separated by occasional rocky headlands, stretches all the way from the north side of Ouranoupolis's small harbour to the tiny ferry harbour at **Tripiti**, 8 km (5 miles) northwest of Ouranoupolis. A long beach north of the harbour offers sunloungers, umbrellas and a range of watersports. Several other organised beaches along this stretch of coast provide similar facilities. That said, there are plenty of emptier stretches for those who want more space. South of Ouranoupolis harbour – literally in the shadow of a medieval monastery tower – is another 2-km (1-mile) length of sand and pebble beach.

Offshore, there are sandy beaches on the tiny, uninhabited island of **Drenia**, where several summer tavernas offer fresh fish, sunloungers and umbrellas. 'Water taxi' boats shuttle back and forth from Ouranoupolis harbour all day in high summer (June–Aug).

Ierissos, 16 km (10 miles) northwest of Ouranoupolis on the opposite side of the isthmus, faces north across a wide blue bay and has a 3.2-km

⬗ *A statue of Aristotle stands in Aristotle's Park, near Stageira*

(2-mile) sandy beach plus a plentiful supply of small tavernas and restaurants in summer.

Nea Roda, 6 km (4 miles) east of Ierissos, has a less impressive beach, a small fishing harbour and a row of small shipyards where traditional wooden fishing boats are built and repaired.

THINGS TO SEE & DO

Aristotle's Park
Educational and fun, this park with a difference is dedicated to the discoveries of Aristotle, who was born in nearby Stageira and later became tutor to the young Alexander the Great. Clever displays illustrate how his thinking paved the way for key scientific discoveries. At under an hour's drive from Ouranoupolis, it makes a good day trip.
ⓐ 1 km (½ mile) west of Stageira village, 44 km (28 miles) northwest of Ouranoupolis ☎ 23770 21130 ⓦ www.ierissos.gr ⓛ Dawn until dusk daily

Athos cruises
The spectacular monasteries of the 'Holy Mountain', with their formidable walls and coloured domes, must be seen to be believed. Cruise ships leave daily in summer from Ouranoupolis, allowing you to view the remote monasteries from the sea. Bring binoculars for a closer look. The cruises last for around 3 hours.
Athos Sea Cruises ⓐ Buy tickets near central square, Ouranoupolis
☎ 23770 71071 ⓦ www.athos-cruises.gr ⓛ Sailings 10.30 & 13.45 daily

Dioriga Xerxi (Xerxes Canal)
When the Persian King Xerxes invaded Greece in 480 BC, his army dug a canal across the narrowest point of the isthmus between Nea Roda and Tripiti. Traces of this mighty work of ancient engineering can still be seen at various spots, west of the road between the two villages. Look out for signs pointing to Dioriga Xerxi (Xerxes Canal).
ⓐ 8–10 km (5–6 miles) northwest of Ouranoupolis ⓛ 24 hours

Island-hopping

The tiny island of **Amouliani**, with its little fishing harbour, lies temptingly close to Ouranoupolis and can be visited on an excursion boat from Ouranoupolis harbour or on the shuttle ferry that plies back and forth from Tripiti, 8 km (5 miles) northwest of Ouranoupolis.

Monastery ruins

Just north of the forbidding concrete and barbed wire frontier that protects the monasteries of Athos from the outside world, the ruins of the 10th-century **Zygou Monastery** are slowly being excavated and restored. There is a small, clean beach (no facilities) nearby if you fancy a refreshing dip.

ⓐ 3 km (2 miles) south of Ouranoupolis ⓛ Dawn until dusk daily

O Pyrgos tis Ouranoupolis (Tower of Ouranoupolis)

This picturesque 15th-century monastic tower, which is such a landmark in Ouranoupolis, has been extensively restored and now contains an excellent small museum with a collection of archaeological finds, including ancient bronze helmets, pottery and weapons, as well as an exhibition highlighting the history of Ouranoupolis and Mount Athos, and scale models of some of the amazing monasteries of Athos. The upper floors have been kept as they were when the authors and humanitarian campaigners Sydney and Joice Loch made the tower their home from the 1920s until the 1970s, and have fine views of the coast.

ⓐ Overlooking the harbour in the centre of Ouranoupolis ⓣ 23770 71389 ⓛ 09.00–17.00 daily ⓘ Admission charge

Quad-bike adventure

Many dirt tracks and unsurfaced forest roads lead through the wooded hills around Ouranoupolis, making it ideal for mountain biking, quad biking or motor cycling. Several companies offer bike and quad rental and guided quad safaris.

Fun Adventure ⓣ 69846 04948 ⓦ www.funadventuregreece.gr or www.funadventure.at ⓛ 09.00–13.00, 15.00–20.00 daily (Apr–Sept)

O Pyrgos tis Ouranoupolis (Tower of Ouranoupolis)

◆ *The magic of sunset over Mount Athos*

Scuba diving

Several dive sites for divers of varying levels of skill lie close to Ouranoupolis and around the coast of Sithonia, on the opposite side of the bay. Visibility is excellent, and the waters around Amouliani Island and the islets lying off its southeast are rich in marine life. The luxury Eagle's Palace Hotel (see page 110) offers scuba-diving packages including accommodation. Its dive centre is also open to non-residents.

ⓐ Aqualand, Eagle's Palace Hotel, Ouranoupolis ❶ 69470 74901 ⓦ www.aqualand.gr ⏲ 09.00–19.00 daily (June–Sept) ❶ Admission charge

Virtual Worlds

The **Ierissos Cultural Centre** uses advanced three-dimensional, high-definition technology to take the visitor on a 'virtual visit' to the monasteries of Mount Athos, the rainforests of Australia and the underwater world of a tropical coral reef.

ⓐ Ierissos town centre ❶ 23770 21131 ⓦ www.ierissos.gr ⏲ 09.00–12.00, 15.00–18.00 Mon–Sat ❶ Admission charge

TAKING A BREAK

Drenia ££ This summer taverna serves fresh fish, salads, snacks and cold drinks on an idyllic stretch of sandy beach on Drenia – the tiny, uninhabited island about 2 km (1¼ miles) southwest of Ouranoupolis. Get there by boat, either the one that connects Ouranoupolis with Amouliani, or by private rental boat. ⏲ 11.00–sunset daily (June–Sept)

O Glaros ££ This restaurant on the little island of Amouliani, within sight of Ouranoupolis, serves fresh-caught fish at tables right at the water's edge. ⓐ Amouliani harbour ❶ 23770 51102 ⏲ 11.00–23.00 daily

Kostakos ££ Several tavernas and *ouzeries* cluster around Nea Roda's fishing harbour. Kostakos, specialising in locally caught seafood, is probably the best of the bunch. ⓐ Nea Roda beach, near the harbour ❶ 23770 31032 ⏲ 12.00–15.00, 19.00–23.00 daily

Kritikos ££ Good fresh fish and seafood, traditional oven-cooked dishes and a surprisingly extensive wine list. ⓐ Main beach road, village centre, Ouranoupolis ❶ 23770 71222 ❷ 12.00–15.00, 19.00–23.00 daily

Kamares £££ This superb, upmarket restaurant within the area's most exclusive luxury hotel is worth a visit for a special occasion. The menu is a fine fusion of Greek and modern Mediterranean cuisine and the wine list is extensive. ⓐ Eagle's Palace Hotel, Ouranoupolis ❶ 23770 31101 ⓦ www.eaglespalace.gr ❷ 13.00–16.00, 20.00–23.00 daily (Easter–Sept) ❶ Reservations essential

● *See the sights of ancient Thessaloniki*

 EXCURSIONS
Out & about

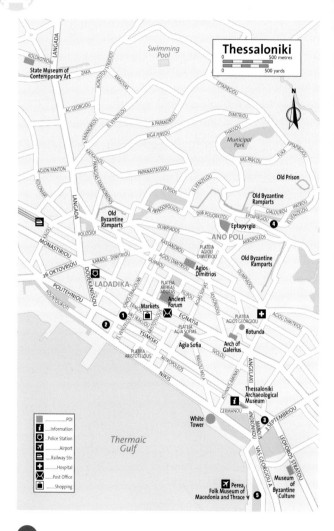

Thessaloniki

Thessaloniki, Greece's second-largest city, is only 30–60 minutes away from the beach resorts of Halkidiki and has a fascinating selection of historical and cultural sights. It is a lively, youthful city, home to one of Greece's largest universities, and has some of Greece's best restaurants, exciting nightlife in the buzzing **Ladadika** area, and an array of World Heritage Sites. Relics of the Roman, Byzantine and Ottoman empires are scattered around its busy streets, and its huge market area is an attraction in its own right. The golden treasures of Macedonian kings are on display in the city's Archaeological Museum, and Thessaloniki also has a collection of fascinating specialist museums.

The city is built around a vast, almost landlocked bay, the Thermaic Gulf, and its streets rise in tiers towards a hilltop crowned with the ruined walls of an ancient fortress, Eptapyrgio. Thessaloniki's main thoroughfare, Egnatia, follows the line of an ancient Roman highway, the Via Egnatia, and its waterfront esplanade, Nikis, is lined with shops and smart cafés. Midway along Nikis, Plateia Aristotelous (Aristotle Square) is an elegant pedestrian square surrounded by café terraces that is the social hub of the city. What makes this vibrant city even better is that most of its main attractions are within easy walking distance of one another.

THINGS TO SEE & DO

Ancient Forum

The Ancient Forum was the heart of Thessaloniki in its 4th-century AD Roman heyday, when it would have been alive with shops, public affairs and services. It is still being excavated and rediscovered, and until the work is complete the remains of its open-air theatre and rows of columns can only be viewed from outside. That said, it is well worth the short walk from Plateia Aristotelous.

ⓐ Plateia Arheas Agoras Ⓦ www.culture.gr Ⓛ Can be viewed from any side of the square 24 hours

Arch of Galerius

Built by the Roman Emperor Galerius in AD 303 to mark his victory over the Persians, this triumphal arch is carved with depictions of battles and Galerius's vanquished enemies.

ⓐ East end of Egnatia ⓛ 24 hours

Byzantine churches

More than a dozen historic Byzantine churches, some of them dating back to the early centuries of the Christian era, stand amid the modern buildings of Thessaloniki. Several are listed as UNESCO World Heritage Sites. Among the most impressive and easiest to visit, as they are located close to the city centre, are the great church of **Agia Sofia** (Holy Wisdom), built in the 8th century, and the huge church of **Agios Dimitrios** (Greece's largest church), also built in the 8th century but completely rebuilt after being destroyed in the great fire that swept through the city in 1917.

ⓐ Agia Sofia, Plateia Agia Sofias and Agios Dimitrios, Plateia Agiou Dimitriou ⓦ www.culture.gr ⓛ 09.00–13.00 Tues–Sun

Eptapyrgio

To discover **Ano Poli** ('the high city'), the oldest and most picturesque part of Thessaloniki, walk uphill from the Rotonda (see page 76) following the line of the old Byzantine ramparts, until you reach the hilltop fortress known as the Eptapyrgio ('seven-towered'). This formidable stronghold dominated the city for almost 1,000 years, and was still used as a prison until 1989. Restoration continues, and above its huge inner gateway can be seen typically Byzantine reliefs of mythical birds and beasts and Ottoman-carved Koranic inscriptions. The entire city and its surroundings can be seen from this hilltop fortress.

Folk Museum of Macedonia and Thrace

This museum's collection of traditional costumes, musical instruments, weapons, jewellery, prints and photos is colourful and eclectic.

ⓐ Vasilissis Olgas 68 ⓣ 23108 30591 ⓛ 09.00–14.00 Fri–Wed
ⓘ Admission charge

◆ *The Roman Arch of Galerius, Thessaloniki*

Museum of Byzantine Culture

Marvellous coloured icons, some of which are more than 1,000 years old, are the jewels in the crown of this museum's dazzling collection.

ⓐ Leoforos Stratou 2 ☏ 23108 68570 Ⓦ www.mbp.gr 🕒 12.30–19.00 Mon, 08.00–19.00 Tues–Sun (Apr–Oct); 10.30–17.00 Mon, 08.00–17.00 Tues–Fri, 08.00–14.30 Sat & Sun (Nov–Mar) ⓘ Admission charge

Rotunda

This massive circular brick building with its tiled domes has undergone many changes since it was built in AD 306 as a mausoleum for Emperor Galerius. A century after his death, it was turned into a Christian church dedicated to St George (Agios Georgios), and after the Ottoman conquest of Greece it became a mosque. The slim minaret that stands beside it is the only one left in Thessaloniki – a city that, until the early 20th century, had many of these Muslim prayer towers. Inside, some of its splendid medieval mosaics have been preserved, and restoration continues.

ⓐ Plateia Agios Georgiou ☏ 23102 45309 Ⓦ www.culture.gr
🕒 09.00–13.00 Tues–Sun

State Museum of Contemporary Art

For a change from the ancient and medieval world, visit this outstanding collection of works by early 20th-century avant-garde Russian artists.

ⓐ Moni Lazariston, Kolokotroni 21 ☏ 23105 89185 Ⓦ www.greekstate museum.com 🕒 14.00–20.30 Mon, 08.00–20.30 Tues–Sun
ⓘ Admission charge

Thessaloniki Archaeological Museum

The golden treasures of ancient Macedonia, recovered from the tombs of Alexander's ancestors at Pella, Veria and Vergina, form the breathtaking centrepiece of this fascinating museum.

ⓐ Manolis Andronikou 6 ☏ 23108 30538 Ⓦ www.macedonian-heritage.gr/Museums 🕒 14.00–20.30 Mon, 08.00–20.30 Tues–Sun
ⓘ Admission charge

White Tower

Standing at the east end of Thessaloniki's waterfront, this 30-m (98-ft) round stone tower is almost 500 years old. It once formed part of the city's defences, and was also used as a prison and place of execution – hence its other nickname, the 'Bloody Tower'. A new history museum was recently opened in the refurbished tower. It presents a view of the history of Thessaloniki, focusing on important moments in the city's past, with multimedia displays.

ⓐ East end of Nikis ❶ 23102 67832 Ⓦ www.mbp.gr ❶ 08.30–15.00 Tues–Sun ❶ Admission charge

TAKING A BREAK

Dozens of smart restaurants, café-bars and clubs can be found in the Ladadika district, a former warehouse area just inland from the harbour that only really comes alive after dark. You will pay a high premium for a drink at one of the cafés around central Plateia Aristotelous, or spend a great deal less in the authentically scruffy *ouzeries* and tavernas in the Vlali market area. Perea, about 18 km (11 miles) south of the city and 6 km (4 miles) from the airport, is where locals go to stroll along the esplanade and eat fresh fish in one of many seaside restaurants.

Ouzou Melathron £ ❶ You can't miss this huge *ouzeri* close to the corner of Tsimiski and El Venizelou – its façade is covered with larger-than-life figures of street performers, including musicians, a mighty weightlifter and a dancing bear. The food is Greek-style *meze* and it's very popular with locals. ⓐ Karpi 21–34 ❶ 23102 75016 Ⓦ www.ouzoumelathron.gr ❶ 12.00–01.00 daily

Zithos £ ❷ This brasserie-style restaurant-bar in the heart of the Ladadika district overlooks a lively square where gypsy musicians perform; it serves a wide choice of beers along with traditional Greek snacks and dishes with a modern twist. ⓐ Katouni 5 ❶ 23105 40284 Ⓦ www.zithos.gr ❶ 11.00–23.00 daily

TOP TIPS FOR VISITING
- Thessaloniki is easily reached by bus from all the Halkidiki resorts. However, you may have to change buses at Nea Moudania.
- Thessaloniki can be visited all year round. However, the weather can be wet, cold and windy from November until early April.
- Several museums are closed or have shorter opening hours on Mondays, and the market area is mostly closed on Sundays. So the best days to visit are Tuesday to Saturday.

Bita ££ ❸ Spotless, stylish, light and airy surroundings (tables inside and out) with a marvellous menu that blends Greek ingredients in new ways. Perfect location for lunch while visiting the Museum of Byzantine Culture and the Thessaloniki Archaeological Museum, which is just across the road. Platters of *ouzo* snacks, cheeses and cold cuts, or à la carte meals. ⓐ 3 Septembriou 2 ⓣ 23108 69695 ⓛ 12.00–15.00 Sun & Mon, 12.00–15.00, 19.00–24.00 Tues–Sat

1900 ££ ❹ This large and well-known *ouzeri* is a good stop for a cold drink and a snack, a longer lunch, or an evening out in the older part of Thessaloniki. ⓐ Kleious 30, Tsinari ⓣ 23102 75462 ⓛ 12.00–16.00, 19.00–01.00 daily

Sea Food £££ ❺ The seafood restaurant of Thessaloniki's poshest hotel is stylish and – depending on what you order – can be surprisingly affordable too. ⓐ Makedonia Palace Hotel, M. Alexandrou 2 ⓣ 23108 97197 ⓦ www.classicalhotels.com ⓛ 12.00–15.00, 19.00–23.00 daily

Mount Athos

The cruise around the unique and spectacular monasteries of the Mount Athos Peninsula is an excursion that no visitor to Halkidiki should miss.

Called Agion Oros (Holy Mountain) in Greek, this is the easternmost of the three Halkidiki peninsulas. At its southern tip it rises to the 2,033-m (6,670-ft) summit of Mount Athos itself, the highest peak in the Halkidiki region. More than 20 self-governing monasteries are dotted around its shores. Many of them stand right on the shoreline and are easy to see from the sea, but some of the oldest and most reclusive foundations are hidden from prying eyes on thickly wooded mountain slopes. Several of these monasteries were founded more than 1,000 years ago, in the golden age of the Byzantine Empire, and today more than 2,000 monks from all over the Orthodox world live here. The monasteries of the west coast are closest to the shoreline and easier to see, so most cruises simply sail south from Ouranoupolis to the southern tip of Athos and back.

🔺 *Agiou Panteleimonos (Roussiko monastery) nestles below the mountainside*

THE MONASTERIES
Zografou & Kastamonitou
Up in the hills, the two northernmost monasteries on the west coast of Athos can barely be glimpsed from the sea. Zografou was founded in 971 and Kastamonitou around a century later, but both were extensively rebuilt in the 18th and 19th centuries.

Docheiariou
Docheiariou's old stone buildings come right down to the waterline and rise inland above a huge arched gateway. Founded in the 10th century, the monastery claims to contain a fragment of the True Cross and an icon of the Virgin Gorgoepekoos to which healing powers are attributed by the devout.

Xenofontos
This is another 10th-century foundation, which was considerably extended in 1837–8.

Agiou Panteleimonos (Roussiko)
Built on the southwest side of the peninsula, Roussiko (or Rousikon) is by far the most picturesque of all the Athos monasteries, with its massive

SUPPORT AND SURVIVAL
The monasteries of Mount Athos thrived better under the Turks than after Greek independence. They owned huge farms, vineyards and olive groves throughout Halkidiki, and in the 18th and 19th centuries many of them were enriched by endowments and bequests from the devoutly Orthodox tsars and nobles of Russia. However, during the notorious 'exchange of populations' after the war (against Turkey) of 1922–3, the Greek government seized many of the monastery estates on Sithonia and Kassandra in order to re-settle Greek refugees from Asia Minor.

12th-century walls crowned by onion-domed churches. As its name implies, this monastery had (and still has) close links with the Russian Orthodox Church.

Simonos Petras

Barely visible from the sea, this 14th-century monastery stands on a rocky ridge to which its founder was reputedly drawn by a ghostly light.

Grigoriou

Another 14th-century foundation, Grigoriou perches above the sea on a tree-covered crag. Destroyed by fire in 1761, it was then completely rebuilt.

Agiou Dionysiou

Agiou Dionysiou's buildings sit at the top of 80-m (260-ft) cliffs. Although its location is spectacular, it is one of the more recent monasteries, having been built within the last 500 years.

TOP TIPS FOR CRUISING

- Take binoculars for a closer look at the monasteries from your boat and your most powerful zoom lens for photography.
- April–May and Sept–Oct, take a light jacket, fleece or sweater. June–Sept, a hat, sunglasses and sunblock are essential.
- Cruise boats leave daily in summer from Ouranoupolis and from Ormos Panagias, on the east coast of Sithonia 6 km (4 miles) northwest of Vourvourou. Drinks and snacks are sold on board.
- Cruises last about 3 hours (from Ouranoupolis) to 4 hours (from Ormos Panagias).

Athos Sea Cruises 🄰 Buy tickets near central square, Ouranoupolis 🄲 23770 71071 🅦 www.athos-cruises.gr

Ormos Travel 🄰 Ormos Panagias 🄲 23750 31522 🅦 www.halkidiki.com/ormos-travel

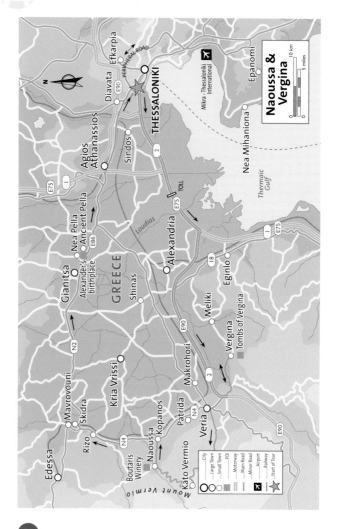

Naoussa & Vergina

Within an hour's drive west of Thessaloniki around the rural town of Naoussa and the green foothills of Mount Vermio lie some of Greece's most highly regarded vineyards and the home of one of Greece's oldest winemaking dynasties. On the way, you can stop at some of the most striking archaeological sites in the region, including the birthplace of Alexander the Great, and the tombs and treasures of his ancestors (see tour on map, page 82). This part of Greece, where the hills meet the coastal plains, is green and fertile compared with the lowlands. In fact, Naoussa, like other towns here, even has cool streams trickling through the town centre, and fresh trout is usually on the menu in the local tavernas.

THINGS TO SEE & DO

Tombs of Vergina

The bones discovered here by Professor Manolis Andronikos in 1977 seem certain to be those of Philip II of Macedon, father of Alexander the Great. Together with other discoveries from the site, they confirm that this was Ancient Aigai, the earliest capital of Macedon. Go to the cavernous Royal Tombs and the nearby Macedonian Tombs before visiting the underground on-site museum, with its treasure trove of golden finds, including the amazing *larnax* (funerary chest), emblazoned with Philip's Macedonian sun-symbol, which contained his bones and skull.

🅐 Vergina, 12 km (8 miles) southeast of Veria 🕿 23310 92347
🕐 12.00–19.00 Mon, 08.00–19.30 Tues–Sat (Apr–Oct); 08.30–15.00 Tues–Sun (Nov–Mar) 🛈 Admission charge

Boutaris Winery

The Boutaris family have been making wine since 1879 and are among Greece's largest producers. For more than a century, sheer volume allowed Boutaris to dominate the market, but since the 1990s the company has also moved into making very high-quality varietals, and has begun to break into international markets and win major awards.

Enjoy an audiovisual show, visit the vineyards and taste some Boutaris vintages to be convinced.

ⓐ Stenimahos, Naoussa ⓣ 23320 59700 ⓦ www.boutari.gr

ⓛ By appointment

Alexander's birthplace

Slender white stone columns mark the site of Ancient Pella, capital of Philip II of Macedon and the birthplace of his son, Alexander the Great. At first sight, there is little to indicate that this was a great city of the ancient world. But enter the site to discover stunning and superbly preserved mosaics made from perfectly matched white, red, black and yellow pebbles, depicting scenes from Greek mythology. Founded in the 5th century BC, Pella fell into decline after Alexander's death. It was sacked by the Romans in 168 BC, and by the end of the 2nd century AD it had vanished from history, only to be rediscovered by 20th-century archaeologists. There is clearly more to be unearthed: in 2006, a local farmer discovered the largest tomb ever found in Greece – that of a

ⓐ One of the beautiful mosaics at ancient Pella

noble family from the 3rd or 2nd century BC, complete with funerary statues, murals and inscriptions.

The site straddles the E86 road, which follows the line of the Via Egnatia, the great Roman highway which connected Igoumenitsa on the west coast of Greece with Thessaloniki and Constantinople.

TAKING A BREAK

Oinomageiremata £ Popular traditional taverna just a short walk downhill from the main square in Naoussa. ❷ St Dragouni 1 & Venizelou, Naoussa ❶ 23320 23576 ❸ 12.00–15.00, 19.00–22.00 Tues–Sun

TOP TIPS FOR ROAD TRAVEL

Rent a car at your resort to make the most of this trip. To avoid the heavy traffic in central Thessaloniki, follow the ring road around the city (clearly signposted 'Peripheral Road'). Where this meets the E75/E90/N1 highway, take the exit signposted Katerini.

Where the E90 and the E75 (A1) diverge, veer right on the E90 (west) and continue for about 40 km (25 miles). Take the exit for Vergina and Veria (route 4). After 10 km (6 miles) turn left to Vergina. The archaeological site of Ancient Vergina is about 2 km (1¼ miles) south of the village centre.

Leave Vergina by route N4, cross the E90 highway, and head towards Veria. Turn left off the N4 just before you reach Veria to follow the winding road to Naoussa through some spectacular mountain scenery. From Naoussa, return to the N4 (follow signs to Kopanos) and head north, following signs to Edessa and Mavrovouni. At Mavrovouni, turn on to the E86 highway and continue east for about 40 km (25 miles), bypassing Gianitsa and Nea Pella (Modern Pella) on your left. Ancient Pella is just off the main road, clearly sign-posted, about 2 km (1¼ miles) east of Nea Pella.

From Ancient Pella, continue east along the E86 for about 25 km (15½ miles) to return to the Thessaloniki ring road.

Mount Olympus & Dion

Mount Olympus, the legendary home of the Greek pantheon, beckons from the western horizon of Halkidiki, spectacularly silhouetted at sunset from resorts such as Sani that face across the Thermaic Gulf. This 20-km (13-mile) long mountain range, rising to the highest summit in Greece, dominates the east coast of northern Greece, and its slopes are designated as a national park. It's a spectacular part of Greece, where flocks of chamois roam, and vultures and eagles soar above harshly beautiful, arid highlands. The views, even from the lower levels, can be breathtaking – as can the ascent to the peaks. More than 1,400 species of shrubs, herbs and wild flowers can be found on the mountain, and the park shelters numerous rare birds, butterflies and reptiles.

Olympus is surprisingly accessible to any reasonably fit adult – the only key requirement being a good pair of boots. From its slopes, the main coast road and the railway line to Thessaloniki look almost close enough to touch, and on a clear day you can see all the way across the Thermaic Gulf to the coasts of the Kassandra Peninsula and even Mount Athos.

The top of Olympus is frequently cloud-capped, and from the ancient temple-city of Dion, on the plains below the mountain, it is easy to see why the Greeks thought of it as the home of their gods. Although Dion dates from as early as the 4th century AD, most of the ruins here – including the remains of heated baths, a theatre, some excellent mosaics and a Christian basilica – date from the later Roman era. The ponds and channels around the site are home to families of coypus – the descendants of escapees from the fur farms of Kastoria. The small, modern museum in the village has an interesting collection of finds from the sanctuary at Dion dedicated to the Roman–Egyptian goddess Isis.

ⓐ Dion, 8 km (5 miles) west of main E75/N1 motorway ⓣ 23510 53206
ⓛ 12.00–19.00 Mon, 08.00–19.30 Tues–Sat (Apr–Oct); 08.30–15.00 Tues–Sun (Nov–Mar) ⓘ Admission charge

TOP TIPS FOR CLIMBING ROUTES

• Allow two days and nights to climb to the summit of Olympus and return. If you have only one day, you could try the journey from the foot of the hill to the bunkhouse taverna at around 2,000 m (6,562 ft) and back; it should take 6–8 hours, allowing time for lunch or a picnic.

Try this walking route, which requires two overnight stops and is probably the easiest. Except for the final traverse to the 2,917-m (9,571-ft) summit of Mitikas, across a short but knife-edged ridge with steep drops on either side, no technical skills or equipment are needed in summer.

• Start from the car park about 5 km (3 miles) west of Litochoro village, around 1,000 m (3,280 ft) above sea level.

• From here, make the steep zigzag hike through pine-wooded canyons to the alpine refuge at around the 2,000-m (6,562-ft) level (allow 3–4 hours).

• Stay overnight at the refuge – which has a bunk-bedded dormitory and its own taverna.

• Then allow 6–8 hours to trek to the summit and back the following day.

• Stay a second night at the refuge, returning to your car the following morning.

🛈 You'll need a small day-pack, good hillwalking footwear, sunblock, a hat, and for the walk to the summit you should allow at least 2 litres of water per person.

🛈 The walk should not be attempted alone, and only skilled and well-equipped mountaineers should consider it in winter.

🛈 Litochoro is around 100 km (62 miles) south of Thessaloniki and is easily accessible by train or bus. You can take a taxi from the railway station (on the coast, 8 km/5 miles from Litochoro village) to the car park at the foot of Olympus and arrange for one to pick you up after your descent.

SUMMIT STATS

Amazingly, there is no record of anyone reaching the top of Mitikas – the summit of Mount Olympus – until the 20th century, although an Ottoman sultan reputedly had a go in the 16th century. The first to reach the summit were Christos Kakalos, from Greece, and two Swiss climbers, Frederic Boissonas and Daniel Bau-Bovy, in 1913.

🔺 *Spectacular view of Mount Olympus*

Skiathos & Skopelos

On a clear day, you can just see the silhouettes of some of Greece's prettiest islands from the southern shores of the Kassandra and Sithonia peninsulas, a little over 100 km (62 miles) away. Skiathos, the main island of the Sporades group, has super sandy beaches, clear blue water and pine-wooded hills. Its main (and only) village, also called Skiathos, is a postcard-pretty spot where the gleaming motor cruisers of Greek shipping millionaires moor next to sailing yachts and wooden fishing vessels. Neatly kept houses with red-tiled roofs and balconies made colourful by potted geraniums and bougainvillea rise in tiers above tranquil twin harbours, where a miniature Venetian fortress is a reminder of more turbulent times. Skopelos – Skiathos's larger but quieter neighbour – lies just a few kilometres away.

SKIATHOS

Skiathos's main village (like almost all Greek island capitals) is normally just called **Chora** – which means simply 'the village'. Built in the early 1830s (after the island's inhabitants finally decided to relocate to the coast from the less convenient but more secure mountains inland), the houses' red-tiled roofs and village church with its campanile make the village look almost more Italian than Greek. It has some interesting shopping – including a number of small ceramics studios and shops specialising in island lace and embroidery. The long quayside forms a

GETTING THERE

Fast hydrofoil services operate (May–Sept only) from Neos Marmaras, Pefkohori, Porto Carras, Nea Moudania and Thessaloniki to the Sporades islands (Skiathos and Skopelos). Operators and timetables change from season to season. For timetables and bookings while in Halkidiki, visit ⓦ www.gtp.gr or www.greeka.com, or book through travel agencies in any of the larger resorts.

⬤ The bell tower in Chora, Skiathos

double crescent, with the smarter cafés and restaurants along the western half of the harbour.

Inland from the harbour (signposted from the quayside), the **Papadiamantis Museum** celebrates the life and work of the island's most famous son, the short-story writer Alexandros Papadiamantis (1851–1911). His statue also presides over a graceful neoclassical concert hall on Bourtzi, a tiny island just offshore fortified by the Venetians during the 17th century. Now linked to the waterfront by a causeway, it is used for open-air concerts on summer evenings.

In the hills above Chora (8 km/5 miles from the village), the 'ghost village' of **Kastro** was the island's main settlement until Greek victory in the war of independence made the islands safe from Turkish raiders and the islanders moved to Chora to build a new home. In medieval times, the village was home to more than 1,000 people and had 22 churches. Today, it is deserted and only two of the churches remain. The most interesting is **Pantokrator**, which contains some excellent Byzantine frescoes and icons.

Papadiamantis Museum ⓐ Town centre, signposted ① 24270 23843 ⓛ 09.00–13.30, 17.00–20.30 Tues–Sun

Church of Pantokrator ⓐ Kastro ⓛ Normally dawn until dusk daily

SKOPELOS

The main village of Skopelos is also called Chora. However, it looks very different from Skiathos, with streets of sturdy traditional houses with jutting wooden balconies and roofs of grey stone slabs. Skopelos is full of character, with tavernas and cafés under the shade of pines and tamarisk trees lining a long seaside promenade. Less well known than its sister-island, Skopelos gained its turn in the limelight in 2008, as the location for the film *Mamma Mia!*, which triggered a small tourism boom. At the highest point of the village are the scant remains of a tiny Venetian castle, but Skopelos's must-see location is **Moni Evangelistrias**, the 18th-century convent where the nuns sell handmade embroidery, textiles, plus jams and honey from their own gardens and beehives. The village also has a small **Folk Art Museum**, where 18th- and 19th-

century furniture and local costumes are on show inside a gracious 19th-century town house.

TAKING A BREAK

Karnayio £££ The island's top restaurant has won numerous awards and serves a blend of Greek and Italian cooking such as rigatoni with smoked salmon, penne with Parma ham, and excellent seafood. ⓐ Paraliaki Skiathou, Chora ❶ 24270 22868 🕒 12.00–15.00, 19.00–24.00 daily (Easter–Oct)

⏵ *Getting ready for another day in Halkidiki*

LIFESTYLE
The Halkidiki way

Food & drink

EATING HABITS

Greeks tend to breakfast lightly and dine late; when going out to a restaurant few Greeks would consider sitting down to dinner earlier than 21.00. In tourist areas such as Halkidiki, the choice of places to eat is wide and cosmopolitan, ranging from traditional tavernas to fast-food joints, pizzerias, restaurants serving a range of modern Mediterranean and international cuisine, and even Indian and Chinese restaurants. Thessaloniki has some of Greece's most sophisticated restaurants, but some of the best food in Greece can be discovered in little old-fashioned *ouzeries* scattered around its backstreets.

Restaurants specialising in grilled meat dishes – usually lamb, chicken and pork, grilled on the spit – are known as *psistaria*, while a seafood restaurant is known as a *psarotaverna*. In such restaurants, you choose your fish, which is then weighed in front of you and priced accordingly. An *ouzeri* or *mezedopolion* serves Greece's national spirit (by the glass or bottle), plus wine or beer, with an array of snacks and small dishes. A *kafeneion* is a traditional café that serves Greek-style coffee, instant coffee and sometimes filter coffee, tea (usually served without milk, and in a glass), soft drinks and a limited range of alcoholic drinks. A *zacharoplasteion* is a pastry shop that usually serves coffee and spirits as well as an assortment of sweet and creamy cakes and other desserts. Greece's home-grown fast food is *giros* or *souvlaki*, lamb grilled on the spit and served with vegetables, chips and yoghurt in pitta bread.

LICENSING HOURS, SMOKING & OPENING TIMES

All Greek eating places serve alcohol at all times. It's not unusual in an old-style café in a market district or beside a fishing harbour to see traders or fishermen who have been at work since before dawn enjoying a shot of *ouzo* with their morning coffee. A smoking ban in enclosed public spaces was introduced in 2002 but has been largely ignored; however, restaurants are required to provide non-smoking tables.

Cafés in towns and cities usually open around 08.00 or earlier to cater for early rising workers; they stay open until 24.00 or later. Cafés in resort areas open around 09.00 or 10.00. Most restaurants open 12.00–15.00 for lunch, then close until at least 19.00 before reopening for dinner until around midnight. In summer, many establishments stay open as late as 02.00.

LOCAL FOOD

Halkidiki and Thessaloniki have some of the best and most varied food in Greece. The region has fertile farmland, so there is never a shortage of farm-fresh fruit and vegetables, from figs and watermelons to sun-ripened tomatoes, peppers, courgettes and aubergines.

🔺 Fresh mackerel, on sale in the market

The long coastlines of Halkidiki and the shallow waters of the Thermaic Gulf provide a superb choice of seafood, from anchovies and sardines to tuna, grouper, red mullet and sea bream to prawns, mussels and other shellfish, lobster, squid and octopus. More unusual seafoods include sea urchins, which are found in huge numbers around Greece's coasts. Unlike most of Greece, the region is also well supplied with fresh fish such as trout, carp, bream and eel from the lakes and rivers of northern Greece.

Meat is usually grilled, and lamb, chicken and pork are favoured. Typically, Greek dishes served in traditional grill restaurants include roasted sheep's head (complete with eyeballs) or *kokoretsi*, a confection of sheep's liver, kidney and other offal bound together with intestines, then grilled on the spit. Greek cuisine also features many oven-cooked dishes, which are simmered slowly in oil for hours. These include the ever-popular *moussaka*, made with minced lamb layered with aubergine and béchamel sauce. Other oven dishes include *giouvetsi* (meat baked in a clay pot with pasta), *kleftiko* (lamb sealed in foil and greaseproof paper and slow-roasted) and *stifado* (pork simmered in red wine and onions).

Greeks rarely drink alcohol unless accompanied by food, and a glass of *ouzo*, wine or beer usually comes with a complimentary saucer of sunflower seeds, olives, cubes of cheese or slices of sausage, known collectively as *meze* or *poikilia*.

VEGETARIANS

Vegetarians who are happy to live on salad, fresh fruit and cheese for a while will find themselves well catered for in Greece, and the traditional Greek salad is a meal in its own right. To order it without cheese, ask for *angourodomatasalata*. There are also a number of vegetable dips, such as *tsatsiki*, made from garlic, yoghurt and cucumber, and *fava*, made from pureed beans. Cooked vegetable dishes include peppers or tomatoes stuffed with rice and herbs, broad beans in tomato sauce, vegetable stews such as *fasolakia* (made with green beans) and *papoutsakia* (baked aubergine), as well as delicious cheese or spinach pies made with filo pastry (*tyropita* and *spanikopita*).

DESSERTS & SWEETS

Visitors with a sweet tooth find themselves in heaven in Greece, where pastry shops serve a mouthwatering choice of sticky cream and chocolate cakes, plus pastries such as *baklava*, *loukoumadhes* and *kataifi*, filled with custard and *bougatsa*, flavoured with honey, nuts and spices .

DRINKS

Greek wine has improved enormously in recent years, with wineries all over the mainland producing red, white and rosé wines that bear comparison with the products of better-known winemaking countries. Some of the best come from the northern vineyards of Naoussa, northwest of Thessaloniki and from the Carras winery on Sithonia. Retsina, the resin-flavoured white wine of Greece, is cheap but is also an acquired taste; even Greeks sometimes mix it with lemonade or cola.

Another acquired taste is Greece's national spirit, *ouzo*, which is strongly flavoured with aniseed and turns cloudy when mixed with ice or water. *Tsipouro*, a grappa-like spirit, is usually drunk neat, in tiny glasses, after a meal. Greek brandy is on the sweet side but is a pleasant evening tipple. Several brands of lager-style beer are made in Greece, and a wide range of imported wines, beers and spirits is offered everywhere, as are all the well-known international soft drink brands.

Greek tap water is safe to drink, but is often heavily chlorinated, and mineral water is for sale everywhere.

FETA FEUD

From being a purely Greek delicacy, feta has gained worldwide popularity and much of it is now made in dairy-producing countries such as Denmark and the Netherlands. Greece, however, has campaigned for the European Union to ban foreign farmers from designating their cheeses as feta, claiming the label should apply exclusively to cheeses made from the milk of Greek sheep or goats.

Menu decoder

Here are some of the drinks and dishes you might encounter while
visiting the area.

GENERAL

Bira Beer
Frappé Iced coffee
Gala Milk
Kafe (elliniko) Coffee
(Greek)
Kafe (gallico) Coffee (filter)
Krasi Wine
Meli Honey
Nero (metalliko) Water
(mineral)
Nes Instant coffee
Pagota Ice cream
Patates tiganites Chips
Psomi Bread
Tsai Tea
Tyri Cheese
Yiaourti Yoghurt

TYPICAL GREEK DISHES

Dolmades Vine leaves
stuffed with rice, herbs
and maybe meat
Fasolakia Stewed green
beans
Gemista Stuffed tomatoes
Gigantes Stewed broad
beans in tomato sauce

Giouvetsi Meat slow-
cooked in a clay pot with
pasta
Horiatiki Salad of onions,
tomatoes, cucumber,
pepper and feta cheese
Keftedhes Meatballs
Kleftiko Roast lamb
Kokoretsi Grilled offal
Kolokythakia tiganita Fried
courgettes
Melitsanes tiganites Fried
aubergines
Moussaka Minced lamb
baked with aubergines in
béchamel sauce
Paidakia Lamb chops
Papoutsakia Baked
aubergine stuffed with
onion and tomato
Pastitsio Macaroni pie
Psarosoupa Fish soup
Soutsoukakia Meat patties
Spanakopitses Spinach pie
Stifado Pork stewed in red
wine and onions
Tyropitakia Cheese pie

MENU ITEMS & COOKING TERMS

In all the resorts in Halkidiki, restaurant menus are multilingual, although the translations from Greek into English can sometimes be eccentric. For example, it is not unusual for a menu to feature 'fried squits' (squid) 'lamp shops' (lamb chops) or even 'smashed bowels in roasted spit' (*kokoretsi*).

Ahini Sea urchin
Alati Salt
Angouro Cucumber
Arni Lamb
Astakos Langouste (spiny lobster)
Avga Eggs
Barbounia Red mullet
Domata Tomato
Elies Olives
Garidhes Prawns
Glyka Sweets
Horta Boiled greens
Kalamares Squid
Kapnisto Smoked
Karpousi Watermelon

Katsiki Goat
Kotopoulo Chicken
Lahanika Vegetables
Lavraki Sea bass
Maridhes Whitebait
Mayeirefta Oven-cooked
Mydhia Mussels
Oktapodhi Octopus
Piponi Honeydew melon
Psari Fish
Scharas Grilled
Thalassina Seafood
Tiganita Fried
Tsipoura Gilthead bream
Ximo Juice
Xirino Pork

LIFESTYLE

Shopping

The resorts of Kassandra and Sithonia have a plethora of stores peddling colourful tourist items and beach accessories but there is a shortage of shops selling anything really worth taking home. The exception is the luxury Sani Resort, where flashy designer boutiques cluster around the marina.

MARKETS

Thessaloniki's entertaining market area sprawls across several blocks of the city centre. It's a colourful spectacle, with dozens of stalls piled high with brightly coloured flowers, fruit and vegetables, tubs and sacks of herbs, spices and olives, and weird-looking seafood on beds of crushed ice. Old-style tavernas around the market area serve great Greek food at bargain prices.

The oldest market hall is the **Bezesteni**, close to the corner of Solomou and El Venizelou, built in 1459 and instantly recognisable with its six-domed roof. The **Vlali** area is the city's main produce market. It's a great place to shop for picnic materials or for Greek produce such as olives, herbs and handicrafts. The **Modiano** market, housed in a neoclassical hall built in 1922, has some of the city's best delicatessens and traditional tavernas. All three markets open early (around 08.00)

FURS

Most visitors to Halkidiki and Thessaloniki will find the numerous shops selling fur coats and jackets depressing and distasteful. Greece's fur trade centres on Kastoria, west of Thessaloniki, which has a thriving trade in patchwork garments made from offcuts of imported fur. However, many shops also trade quite flagrantly in clothes made from the skins and furs of wild and endangered species such as lynx and ocelot, and the Greek government has shown little interest in enforcing international curbs on the trade.

and are open every day except Sunday and public holidays. They are at their best first thing in the morning, with most shops and stalls closing by 17.00 at the latest.

WORRY BEADS

Many older Greek men still habitually carry a string of *komboloi*, or 'worry beads'. These are traditionally made from coloured glass or ceramic, bone, lapis lazuli, amber, ivory or other semi-precious materials. Genuine antique *komboloi* are sought after by collectors and command high prices, but beautiful modern replicas in a variety of materials can be found at **Komboloi Gallery** (ⓐ Kivelis 5, Thessaloniki ⓦ www.greekkomboloi.com ⓒ 09.00–13.00, 15.00–19.00 daily).

⬥ Colourful produce in the Vlali market

LIFESTYLE

Children

BEACHES

Most beaches in the Halkidiki region are sandy, clean and reasonably safe for children, but not all beaches have lifeguards on duty. For families with toddlers, the best beach resort is **Vourvourou** (see pages 51–3), on the east coast of Sithonia, with its sandy beach and very calm, shallow bay.

ORGANISED ACTIVITIES & CHILD-MINDING

The **Sani Resort** (see pages 42–50) on Kassandra offers a range of sports and other activities for children, ranging from finger-painting and storytelling for toddlers to professional tennis coaching, paintball, mountain biking, horse riding and watersports. The resort also has a children's beach club where child-minders can take care of babies and children for up to 30 minutes a day free of charge.

RESTAURANTS

Children are welcome in all restaurants in the Halkidiki resorts, but few of them provide special facilities for youngsters or child-specific menus. Adventurous children may be fascinated by the Greek habit of cooking and serving fish dishes complete with head, tail and bones. For the less adventurous eaters, there are plenty of places serving pizzas, pasta and burgers.

SCUBA DIVING

With calm seas, excellent underwater visibility and dive sites close to shore, Halkidiki is a good place for children who are competent swimmers to learn to dive. PADI-certified dive centres such as **Triton Scuba Club** at Kallithea (see page 22), **Dive Club Kassandra** at Hanioti (see page 28) and **Sea World Scuba Diving Centre** also at Hanioti (see page 28), offer PADI training courses for children aged 10 and up.

SHOPPING

Small supermarkets in all the resorts meet everyday needs such as sunblock, nappies and baby lotions, and there are plenty of gift shops selling children's clothes and beach accessories.

WATERLAND

This water park at Tagarades, 8 km (5 miles) south of Thessaloniki, has three pools, including a children's pool with lifeguards and Europe's largest splash pool, and a range of slides and rides.

WATERSPORTS

Almost all the Halkidiki resorts have a choice of watersports for older children, including pedalos and canoes. However, lifejackets and supervision are not always provided, and children should always be accompanied by an adult.

◯ Children can have tennis lessons at the Sani Resort

Sports & activities

BIRDWATCHING

The huge, artificial **Lake Volvi**, about 80 km (50 miles) north of Nea Moudania, attracts large numbers of migratory birds, including pelicans, flamingos, herons, cormorants and numerous other waterfowl. Another magnet for migrants is the shallow delta of the **River Axios**, about 16 km (10 miles) southwest of Thessaloniki.

GOLF

The **Porto Carras Golf Course** on Sithonia is one of the best in Greece. Redesigned by Roya Machary in 2004, it is an 18-hole, par 71 course and is open all year.

ⓘ 23750 71381 **Ⓦ** www.portocarras.com

🔺 *Birdwatchers will enjoy the birdlife at Lake Volvi*

MOUNTAIN BIKING

Mountain bikes can be rented at the Sani Resort, on Kassandra, which also offers guided cycling tours for individuals, groups and families.
ⓐ Sani Resort ⓣ 23740 99400 ⓦ www.sani-resort.com

RIDING

Horse-riding excursions are available from the Sani Resort (ⓣ 23740 99400 ⓦ www.sani-resort.com) and from the Porto Carras Resort (ⓦ www.portocarras.com), which has its own stables.

SCUBA DIVING

The waters around Kassandra and Sithonia offer some of the best diving in Greece for novice and experienced divers. Visibility is excellent and there is a lot to see – from the wreck of the MV *Mitilini* just 10 minutes offshore to caves and reefs where divers can see big groupers, moray eel, octopus and sometimes even dolphins. Dive centres include:

Dive Club Kassandra See page 28.
Odyssey Dive See page 35.
Sea World Scuba Diving Centre See pages 28 & 45.
Triton Scuba Club See page 22.

SPAS

Natural hot springs feed the pools and therapeutic baths of the modern resort **Loutra Spa**, near the southern tip of Kassandra. Heated pools, sauna, hammam, hydromassage and specialist treatments are available.
ⓐ Loutra ⓣ 23740 71358

TENNIS

The Sani Beach Hotel has courts and provides coaching (see page 45).

WATERSPORTS

There are watersports centres at all the main resorts on Kassandra and Sithonia. Pedalos, kayaks, catamarans, windsurfers, jet-skis and waterskis are available.

Festivals & events

Details of events in Thessaloniki are available from the Thessaloniki Tourism Organisation (☏ 23102 91638 ⓦ www.thessaloniki.travel) and from major hotels and municipal tourist offices in resorts.

MARCH/APRIL
Easter

The Greek Orthodox **Easter** is a movable feast with dates that can be up to three weeks earlier or later than the Western Easter. It is Greece's most important religious festival, with processions to the great churches of Thessaloniki and to smaller village churches led by priests in gorgeously coloured and embroidered robes, looking like something straight out of an ancient Byzantine past. The high point is midnight on Easter Saturday, when fireworks celebrate the rising of Christ.

⬤ *The magic of a candlelit Greek Orthodox Easter celebration*

MAY

Protomagia (May Day/Labour Day), 1 May

May Day is a typically Greek mix of pagan and Christian tradition and modern politics, when families pick wild poppies and other flowers to weave into garlic wreaths which are hung above doorways to fend off evil spirits. Meanwhile, left-wing parties and trade unions rally in cities and major towns to keep the red flag flying.

MAY/JUNE

The four-day **Thessaloniki Book Fair** is a major event in the city. Most books being presented are in Greek, but visitors with a real interest in the country's culture and natural history can also find fiction and non-fiction in English translations that are hard to find at home.
ⓐ HELEXPO, Egnatias 45, Thessaloniki ☎ 21092 00327
ⓦ www.thessalonikibookfair.com

JULY/AUGUST

Early July–early August

Nea Moudania hosts its annual **Festival of the Sea** with performances of classical and traditional music and Greek drama in the town's open-air theatre, next to the waterfront, throughout the summer.
☎ 23730 21370

Mid-July–end August

The Halkidiki Amphitheatre at Siviris, 8 km (5 miles) west of Kalithea, is the venue for the **Kassandra Festival** of classical and contemporary Greek music and light opera held in the open air.
☎ 23740 23997 ⓦ www.festivalkassandras.com

Mid-July–end August

The luxury Sani Resort hosts the annual **Sani Festival** with six weeks of classical music, world music, jazz and contemporary dance.
☎ 23740 99400 ⓦ www.sani-resort.com

Koimisis tis Theotokou (Assumption of the Virgin), 15 August

Millions of Greeks from the cities and from overseas return to their ancestral villages for *Koimisis*, the biggest family event in the Greek calendar.

NOVEMBER
Mid-November

The **Thessaloniki International Film Festival** hosts screenings of Greek and international new films, documentaries, shorts and archive classics, as well as masterclasses by some of the world's great actors and directors.

☎ 21087 06000 🌐 www.filmfestival.gr

DATES FOR *YOUR* DIARY!

Easter, *Protomagia* and *Koimisis* can all present challenges for anyone planning to travel within Greece around these dates.

- Many bars and restaurants close over Easter, or open just for limited hours.
- Workers' organisations often choose *Protomagia* for strikes and demonstrations that can bring cities such as Thessaloniki and Athens grinding to a halt.
- With millions of people on the move, train, plane, bus and ferry tickets are hard to find around *Koimisis*, and there are often long tailbacks on roads from Thessaloniki to Sithonia and Kassandra.
- Accommodation is at a premium around Easter and *Koimisis*, and anyone planning to travel within Greece around this time needs to make arrangements well in advance.

▶ *The Sani Resort's luxury hotels are built around Sani Marina*

PRACTICAL INFORMATION
Tips & advice

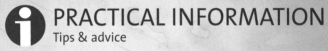

Accommodation

Almost all hotels in Halkidiki close from late October until the Greek Easter (usually April, sometimes May). Some do not reopen until May. Hotels in Thessaloniki stay open all year. The prices below are based on the average price for a double room with bed and breakfast:

£ = under €80   ££ = €80–€150   £££ = more than €150

ATHOS

Hotel Akrogiali £ Affordable small hotel opposite the historic tower and the beach and conveniently close to the harbour and bus stop in the centre of Ouranoupolis. ⓐ Paralia, Ouranoupolis ⓣ 23770 71201

Skites ££ This small collection of pretty bungalow-rooms (some with basic kitchenette) is the best place to stay in Ouranoupolis, with great food, a pool and access to a pebbly beach. ⓐ Ouranoupolis, 1 km (½ mile) south of village centre ⓣ 23770 71140 ⓦ www.skites.gr ⓛ Easter–Oct, closed Nov–Easter

Eagles Palace Resort & Spa £££ This superb luxury hotel stands in glorious isolation a short distance north of Ouranoupolis, on its own beach, with a range of watersports including scuba diving and windsurfing, a private sailing yacht and motor cruisers available for hire. There is a choice of gourmet restaurants, a beach bar and a nightclub. The award-winning spa has a range of therapies and massage treatments on offer. Rooms and suites are spacious, lavishly equipped and have fabulous views. ⓐ 4 km (2½ miles) north of Ouranoupolis ⓣ 23770 31047 ⓦ www.eaglespalace.gr ⓛ Easter–Oct

KASSANDRA

Petrino Suites ££ This beautifully designed hotel has 28 split-level suites in a traditional-style stone house around a shared pool (two suites have private pools) and has an excellent restaurant. ⓐ Afytos, Kallithea ⓣ 23740 91636 ⓦ www.petrino-hotel.gr

Sani Resort £££ The Sani Resort offers a range of luxury suites, villas, bungalows and 4- and 5-star rooms, more than a dozen bars and restaurants, and an outstanding choice of sports and leisure activities. ⓐ Sani ⓣ 23740 99500 ⓦ www.sani-resort.com ⓛ Easter–Sept

SITHONIA

Ekies ££ Simply the best, friendliest and prettiest holiday hotel in the whole of Halkidiki, Ekies has stylish, designer-decorated rooms beside a sandy beach and a blue lagoon of warm, shallow water. There's a pool, a bar, a superb restaurant and a range of activities including yoga. You won't want to leave. ⓐ Vourvourou ⓣ 23750 91000 ⓦ www.ekies.gr ⓛ Easter–Sept

Kelyfos Holiday Resort ££ Comfortable, mid-range resort hotel located a short distance from Neos Marmaras, with excellent sea views. ⓐ Neos Marmaras ⓣ 23750 72833 ⓦ www.kelyfos.gr

Porto Carras Resort £££ The legendary Porto Carras is the most luxurious resort complex on Sithonia. It has a private marina, an 18-hole golf course, and a choice of accommodation from 3 star to 5 star in rooms, suites and villas. ⓐ Neos Marmaras ⓣ 23750 77000 ⓦ www.portocarras.gr

THESSALONIKI

Le Palace Hotel ££ This small, central hotel has pretty, comfortable en-suite rooms and serves an excellent buffet breakfast. ⓐ Tsimiski 12 ⓣ 23102 57400 ⓦ www.lepalace.gr

Makedonia Palace £££ The magnificent Makedonia Palace, Thessaloniki's largest and grandest city hotel, stands on the waterfront with fabulous views of the Gulf. It has several excellent restaurants and immaculate service. ⓐ M Alexandrou 2 ⓣ 23108 97197 ⓦ www.classicalhotels.com

Preparing to go

GETTING THERE

By far the easiest way of getting to Halkidiki is by air to Thessaloniki. Most flights are operated by charter airlines owned by big holiday companies. These also offer package holidays including accommodation, transfers to and from airports and sometimes car hire. Booking a package holiday through a tour operator does not have to be more expensive than making your own arrangements – it can often be cheaper and is almost always less time-consuming. Charter airlines fly to Halkidiki between May and mid-October only. **Thomas Cook Airlines** (Ⓦ www.thomascookairlines.co.uk) flies to Thessaloniki between May and September from London Gatwick and Manchester. **Thomson** (Ⓦ www.flights.thomson.co.uk) has a large choice of flights to Thessaloniki from the UK, with departures between May and September from Bristol, East Midlands, London Luton, Manchester and Newcastle.

The only budget airline offering year-round flights to Thessaloniki is **easyJet** (Ⓦ www.easyjet.com) from London Gatwick, though British Airways also operates throughout the year from there, too, and tickets can be cheap.

Many people are aware that air travel emits CO_2, which contributes to climate change. You may be interested in the possibility of lessening the environmental impact of your flight through the charity **Climate Care** (Ⓦ www.jpmorganclimatecare.com), which offsets your CO_2 by funding environmental projects around the world.

It is possible to travel by land and sea from the UK to Halkidiki, but this is much more expensive than flying and takes three to four days each way. Options include travelling by car or train to Ancona in northern Italy, then making a 20-hour ferry crossing to Igoumenitsa in northwestern Greece, and travelling overland across northern Greece.

The 2,700-km (1,677-mile) drive through Germany, Austria, Slovenia, Croatia, Serbia and the Former Yugoslav Republic of Macedonia takes at least four days and involves numerous border crossings. The train journey to Thessaloniki, via Budapest, Bucharest and Sofia, also takes three to four days.

TOURISM INFORMATION

In the UK, the Greek National Tourist Office (GNTO) (ℯ 4 Conduit Street, London W15 2DJ ☎ 020 7495 9300 🅦 www.gnto.co.uk) can provide general information about your visit.

BEFORE YOU LEAVE

There are no mandatory immunisations. If you require a prescription medicine, bring an adequate supply with you as not all the resorts in Halkidiki have fully stocked pharmacies. Sunblock and suntan lotions are also much more expensive in Greece than in the UK, so bring plenty with you. A basic medical kit should include mosquito repellent, antihistamine tablets for stings and bites, and a diarrhoea remedy. ❶ Note that painkillers containing any amount of codeine, available without prescription in the UK, are classified as illegal drugs in Greece.

ENTRY FORMALITIES

UK and Irish nationals require only a passport to enter Greece and may stay as long as they wish. Citizens of EU countries within the Schengen

TRAVEL INSURANCE

Have you got sufficient cover for your holiday? Check that your policy covers you adequately for loss of possessions and valuables, for activities you might want to try – such as scuba diving, horse riding or watersports – and for emergency medical and dental treatment, including flights home if required. The European Health Insurance Card (EHIC) enables you to reclaim the costs of some medical treatment incurred while travelling in EU countries. For information and an application form, enquire at the post office or visit 🅦 www.ehic.org.uk

Agreement need only a national identity card. Citizens of the USA, Canada, Australia, New Zealand and South Africa do not require a visa for a stay of up to 90 days.

Normal EU customs rules apply. Non-EU visitors may bring in 200 cigarettes, 50 cigars or 250 g of tobacco, 1 litre of spirits, 2 litres of wine or liqueurs, 50 ml of perfume and 250 ml of eau de toilette.

MONEY

The euro is the currency and is available in 5, 10, 20, 50, 100, 200 and 500 euro notes. In practice, most establishments do not accept notes in denominations of more than 50 euros. Coin denominations are: 1 cent, 2 cents, 5 cents, 10 cents, 20 cents, 50 cents, 1 euro and 2 euros.

Sterling notes and US dollars, and sterling and dollar traveller's cheques, can easily be exchanged at banks and in hotels (for information about where traveller's cheques are accepted, see Ⓦ www.americanexpress.com/usetc). Travellers from Scotland should carry Bank of England notes, as sterling notes issued by the Royal Bank of Scotland, Bank of Scotland and Clydesdale Bank are not recognised in Greece. Canadian dollars, New Zealand dollars and South African rand may be difficult to exchange, and travellers from these countries are best advised to carry traveller's cheques in euros.

Also recommended is a Cash Passport prepaid debit card preloaded with euros, which can be purchased from banks and post offices before travelling and can be used in most places, including ATMs.

MasterCard and Visa are widely accepted in hotels, shops and restaurants, but most smaller establishments prefer payment in cash. American Express and Diners Club cards are accepted only in larger hotels, expensive shops in major cities, and by most airlines and car-rental agencies.

ATMs (which accept all major debit and credit cards using the Maestro and Cirrus systems) are widely available in Thessaloniki, but are thin on the ground in the smaller resorts on Kassandra and Sithonia. There is also a Visa ATM locator where customers can obtain information about their nearest ATM. Ⓦ www.thomascook.com/cashpassport

ⓘ There is no bureau de change at Thessaloniki airport, but a 24-hour ATM is available.

CLIMATE

The climate of northern Greece is somewhat cooler and wetter all year round than that of the south, and each of the areas covered in this book has a slightly different microclimate. Sithonia, with its high central massif, attracts more cloud and rainfall than low-lying Kassandra. Occasional thunderstorms are possible throughout the year, even in July and August. Winters are generally mild but wet, with temperatures rarely falling below 10°C (50°F). Summers are hot, with maximum temperatures of up to 38°C (100°F) in July, the hottest month.

BAGGAGE ALLOWANCE

Baggage allowances vary from airline to airline. There are no hard-and-fast rules on maximum weight for hand luggage and checked-in (hold) luggage, nor for the number of pieces of luggage you may check in. Many airlines now charge extra for hold luggage. Generally, only one piece of carry-on luggage per passenger is permitted. Baggage allowances can usually be found on the 'frequently asked questions' (FAQ) section of each airline's website and should also be clearly listed on your ticket or letter of confirmation. If in doubt, contact the airline directly and ask for written confirmation of your baggage allowance.

● *Beach umbrellas provide respite from the sun*

During your stay

AIRPORTS

The main airport for the region is Thessaloniki, officially known as Alexander the Great Macedonia International Airport. It is 14 km (9 miles) southeast of Thessaloniki city centre and around 56 km (35 miles) northwest of Nea Moudania. Taxis are readily available at all times from the rank outside the arrivals hall. A taxi ride to the city centre takes around 15 minutes. Buses to the city centre leave from immediately outside the arrivals hall and take around 30–40 minutes to central Thessaloniki (see also page 120). Major car-rental companies with rental desks at the airport include Avis, Europcar, Hertz and Sixt.

COMMUNICATIONS

Local and international phone calls can be made from phone booths in the centre of most resorts and cities. These use only prepaid phonecards, which can be bought at post offices and most local shops. Mobile phone users subscribing to UK, Irish and mainland EU networks should experience no problems receiving or making calls anywhere in Greece; however, phones purchased in the USA, Canada, South Africa, Australia and New Zealand may not be able to access local networks.

There are Internet cafés, usually with broadband access, in even the smallest resorts. All large hotels, many smaller hotels and guesthouses have Wi-Fi access for those travelling with a laptop. Large hotels often charge a hefty premium for Wi-Fi access, and it is often much cheaper and more convenient to find an independent Internet café nearby.

Post offices are marked by a prominent circular yellow sign and can be found in most large villages. Stamps can be bought at post offices and in many gift shops and newsagents. Airmail letters take three to six days to reach EU countries, five to eight days to the USA and Canada, and slightly longer to Australia, New Zealand and South Africa. Postcards may take several weeks to reach their destination. Post offices are open 07.30–14.00 Monday–Friday.

TELEPHONING GREECE
The country code for Greece is 30. The prefixes for phoning
Greece should be followed by the ten-digit local number.
From the UK, all EU countries and New Zealand: 00 30
From the USA and Canada: 011 30
From Australia: 0011 30

TELEPHONING FROM GREECE
These prefixes should be followed by the city code (minus the
initial 0) and the subscriber's number.
To the UK: 00 44
To the USA or Canada: 001
To Ireland: 00 353
To Australia: 00 61
To New Zealand: 00 64

CUSTOMS
Greeks are, by and large, talkative, hospitable and tolerant towards the
ways of visitors. However, public displays of drunkenness and verbal
aggression are generally considered unacceptable. Thessaloniki airport,
like most Greek airports, is regarded as a security zone and photography,
even of civil aircraft, is forbidden. You may encounter signs forbidding
photography in quite unexpected parts of the coast and at places such
as reservoir dams and major road bridges. Never take photos or videos of
any kind of military installation, unless you want to risk several weeks or
months in jail or a heavy fine.

DRESS CODES
By almost any standard, Greece is a very easy-going country. Jacket and
tie are not required in even the most expensive establishments, and
most Greeks dress for comfort rather than formality – especially in
summer. Topless sunbathing has become acceptable virtually

everywhere. Total nudity is less acceptable except in secluded stretches of beach well away from main resort areas. However, shorts, sleeveless T-shirts and skimpy tops are unacceptable when visiting religious sites such as churches and monasteries, where the modesty code insists on long trousers and at least short-sleeved shirts for men, and a shirt or blouse and over-the-knee skirts or dresses for women.

ELECTRICITY

The voltage in this area is 220 V. Sockets are standard EU, with two round pins. Visitors from the UK and North America will need adaptors, which can be bought in many local shops. Most hotels and guesthouses can lend you an adaptor. Visitors from North America may need a step-down transformer for appliances using 110 V power supply.

EMERGENCIES

Ambulance ☎ 112
General emergency (fire, police and medical) ☎ 112

The main hospitals for the Halkidiki region are in Thessaloniki.
Agios Dimitrios General Hospital ⓐ Zografou 2, Thessaloniki
☎ 23102 03121
Agios Pavlos Hospital ⓐ Plateia Dimokratias, Thessaloniki
☎ 23105 38021
Ahepa General Hospital ⓐ Kyriakidi 1, Thessaloniki ☎ 23109 93111
Georghios Papanikolaou Regional Hospital ⓐ Exohi, Thessaloniki
☎ 23102 57602

Honorary British Consulate ⓐ Tsimiski 43, Thessaloniki
☎ 23102 78006 ⓦ www.fco.gov.uk

GETTING AROUND
Driving conditions

Roads in the region are generally good and traffic outside the Thessaloniki urban area is light except during Greek holiday periods. A four-lane motorway connects Thessaloniki and the airport with Nea Moudania. Recently built, well-surfaced roads connect all major points on Kassandra and Sithonia. Speed limits are 50 kph (31 mph) in built-up areas, 80 kph (50 mph) outside built-up areas and 120 kph (75 mph) on motorways.

Local driving habits can be erratic, and visiting drivers should always use caution. Seat belts must be worn. In the event of a breakdown, most car-rental agencies use the services of one of the following organisations:

ELPA (Automobile and Touring Club of Greece) ⓘ 104

Express Service ⓘ 154

Hellas Service ⓘ 157

Car hire

Most major international rental chains have desks at Thessaloniki airport. If you require a car for just a day or two, these offer adequately maintained vehicles and reasonable value for money. But if you need a car for the whole of your stay, it is usually cheaper to rent through a major international company, an airline or your package tour operator before leaving home.

❶ Full collision damage waiver (CDW), personal accident insurance, bail bond and liability cover are essential

❶ A full UK or EU driving licence is valid but non-EU visitors need an international driving licence

Motorcycle & scooter rental

Motorcycles and scooters can be rented by the day or the week from local agencies at most resorts.

❶ Unless you are already a very experienced biker, think twice before renting. Halkidiki's roads, while well surfaced, are very winding, and local drivers show no mercy to two-wheelers. Many visitors are injured each year in motorcycle and scooter accidents

❶ If you do rent a bike or scooter, wear a helmet at all times. Greek laws do not require bikers to wear helmets when riding within towns or villages, and you will see many locals riding without helmets. However, the risk of injury or death is just as high (if not higher) in built-up areas

Motoring offences
Do not drink and drive. Penalties are severe and blood alcohol limits are set very low – one glass of wine or a half-litre of beer will take you over the limit.

❶ Police may impose fines for motoring offences on the spot

Public transport
Public transport is generally good, with buses operating at least hourly services during the day around Kassandra and Sithonia, calling at all resorts and villages on the main roads that loop each peninsula. There are also services at least six times daily between Thessaloniki and Nea Moudania on Kassandra and Nikiti on Sithonia. Tickets are sold from ticket machines on board. These accept exact payment in coins only.

HEALTH, SAFETY & CRIME
Food & drink
Eating and drinking in Greece is as safe as anywhere in Europe. Public-sector healthcare is below European standards.

Healthcare & precautions
Private-sector clinics and privately run hospitals operate to high standards and usually have English-speaking doctors and some English-speaking nursing staff.

For minor medical problems and advice, local health centres and clinics include:

Nea Moudania Health Centre ❶ 23730 21244 ❶ 08.00–12.00, 14.00–20.00 daily
Neos Marmaras Community Clinic ❶ 23750 71208 ❶ 09.00–12.00, 16.00–20.00 Mon–Fri

Greece has no special health risks, but there are a number of minor nuisances that could spoil your holiday. Mosquitoes can be a pest in summer. Most guesthouse and hotel rooms come equipped with plug-in electric mosquito-repellent devices, but using a dab or two of repellent on exposed skin when going out after dark is advisable. On rocky parts of the beach, be careful not to tread on black sea urchins, whose spines can be very painful. In summer, Greek beaches can sometimes be plagued by large numbers of jellyfish (*tsouchtres*), some of which can deliver an irritating but not dangerous sting.

Local insect life can sometimes be intimidating, but the large hornets and blue-black bees that often buzz around your veranda are harmless unless disturbed – leave them alone, and they will return the favour. Scorpions do exist, but are rarely seen; they too are harmless unless disturbed, with a painful but not lethal sting. Greeks detest all snakes and will try to kill them on sight, but in fact Greece has no dangerous snakes, and most of its several species of snake are non-venomous.

Safety & crime

Instances of violent crime against tourists are rare, but as in any holiday destination there is a risk of petty theft and visitors should use normal caution on the beach and in bars and restaurants. Greece has been cited as the Mediterranean destination with the highest levels of alleged sexual assault against young British women. However, it is worth noting that many of the alleged assaults were by young British male visitors, not by Greek men.

The police presence in Halkidiki is low (reflecting low crime levels), but roads are patrolled by police cars and motorcycle police. Most Greek police officers have a basic but not fluent grasp of English. An official 'tourist police' force exists, but is mainly involved with policing hotel and restaurant regulations.

Credit card fraud

This is an increasing problem in Greece. There are few precautions you can take against your card being abused while in Greece, other than making sure you are always present when it is being used. Be suspicious of shops or restaurants where waiters or shop assistants ask to take your card out of your sight for whatever reason; always insist on being present while your card is being charged or authorised. Keep a personal record of all transactions, and scrutinise all charges closely for several months after you return. All major credit card companies offer insurance against credit card fraud and identity theft, and if you do not already have such a policy, consider taking one out before leaving home.

MEDIA

Many bars in Halkidiki resorts offer international satellite TV channels such as Sky Sports and Setanta. Most hotels also have in-room satellite TV, but the choice of English-language channels is usually limited to news channels such as BBC World and CNN. There are no local English-language newspapers, but most British daily and Sunday newspapers, including *The Times*, the *Daily Telegraph*, the *Daily Mail*, the *Daily Mirror* and *The Sun*, can be bought from shops in the larger resorts on the day after publication, and sometimes on the day of publication. The *International Herald Tribune* is also available on some newsstands and in large luxury hotels on the day of publication, and is co-published with an English-language translation of the major Greek national daily *Kathimerini*, so you can catch up on Greek local news as well as international events. If you have a portable shortwave radio, you can receive the BBC World Service on 9.41, 12.09 and 15.07 MHz.

OPENING HOURS

Opening hours in Halkidiki and Thessaloniki, as in all of Greece, are idiosyncratic. Despite government attempts to impose a nationwide regime of opening times for shops, bars, restaurants and other businesses, in practice most private enterprises open and close as they see fit. Banks and post offices generally open from 08.00 until 14.00 Monday to Friday. Most small shops in resorts open around 09.00, close from around 13.00 to 17.00, then reopen until at least 21.00. Restaurants usually open from 12.00 to 15.00 for lunch, then reopen around 19.00 until around 23.00 for dinner.

ETHNIC AND RELIGIOUS HISTORY

In the early 16th century, an enlightened Ottoman sultan encouraged Jews fleeing the murderous oppression of Christianity and the Spanish Inquisition to settle in Thessaloniki, which under Ottoman rule became a multi-ethnic city with one of the largest Jewish populations in the world, along with a large Muslim community. Thessaloniki's Jews had already begun to emigrate to Palestine by the early 19th century, and emigration speeded up after the city was reconquered by Greece in 1912. The 'exchange of populations' that followed Greece's defeat in its war against Turkey in 1922–3 changed the ethnic and religious make-up of northern Greece completely. Several hundred thousand Muslims, including the entire Muslim population of Thessaloniki, were expelled from Greece, while more than a million Orthodox Christians were driven from Turkey. The Greek government confiscated land from several of the wealthy Mount Athos monasteries to settle many of these people in Halkidiki, and almost all the villagers of Kassandra and Sithonia can trace their roots to vanished Greek communities in what is now Turkey.

Some may stay open as late as 01.00. In summer, some open-air dance clubs located well away from resort centres may stay open until 02.00. Opening hours for museums and archaeological sites under the aegis of the Greek Ministry of Culture are erratic, to say the least, and the hours actually in force often bear no relation to the officially published times. However, most museums and archaeological sites are open 08.30–15.00 Tuesday to Sunday and are closed on Mondays.

RELIGION

For all practical purposes, to be Greek is to be Greek Orthodox, and in Halkidiki and Thessaloniki, it is extremely rare to meet anyone who professes any other religion.

TIME DIFFERENCES

Greek time is GMT +3 hours (Mar–Oct), GMT +2 hours (Nov–Feb); US Eastern Standard Time +7 hours, US Pacific Standard Time +10 hours.

TIPPING

Tipping is not mandatory anywhere in Greece. Service is included in restaurants, and it is also normal practice to leave small change on the table when paying cash in bars and cafés – there is no fixed percentage. As elsewhere in the world, hotel porters welcome tips but there is no fixed rate. Taxi drivers do not expect to be tipped.

TOILETS

Public toilets can be found in parks, squares, railway stations, bus terminals and airports. Standards vary widely; those maintained by local municipalities in resort areas are usually clean, as are those at airports, but toilets at bus and railway stations are often not so well kept. Hotel and restaurant toilets are usually clean but often in need of a makeover. In almost all establishments, except for luxury hotels, you should drop used toilet paper in the bin provided, not in the lavatory bowl.

TRAVELLERS WITH DISABILITIES

Four- and five-star hotels, and most three-star hotels used by package holiday companies, can be expected to have some rooms adapted for wheelchair users, as well as reasonable access to facilities in public areas. However, few smaller guesthouses and hotels, banks, restaurants or shops are wheelchair-accessible, and people with disabilities will, in general, find Greece a difficult country in which to travel. Street and pavement services are often cluttered and poorly surfaced and wheelchair ramps are virtually non-existent.

Tourism for all (📞 0845 124 9971 🅦 www.tourismforall.org.uk) provides information for people with disabilities travelling from the UK.

A

accommodation 43–4, 110–11
Agia Paraskevi 35, 40
Agia Sofia (Thessaloniki) 74
Agios Dimitrios (Thessaloniki) 74
Agiou Dionysiou (Mount Athos) 81
air travel 112–13, 115, 116
Amouliani 66
Ancient Forum (Thessaloniki) 73
Ancient Olinthos 15, 17
Ancient Pella 84–5
Arch of Galerius 74
Aristotle's Park 65

B

beaches 8, 15, 20, 24, 26, 34–5, 40,
    43–4, 51, 54, 56, 58, 63, 65, 102
Bezesteni 100
birdwatching 47, 104
boat travel 28, 45, 51, 59, 65, 79, 81, 89,
    113
Bourtzi 91
Boutaris Winery 83–4

C

car hire 119
children 43–5, 102–3
churches 74, 91
climate 113
crime 117, 121–2

D

Dioriga Xerxi (Xerxes Canal) 65
disabilities 124
diving 22, 26, 28, 35, 45, 69, 102, 105
Docheiariou (Mount Athos) 80
Drenia 63
driving 85, 113, 116, 119–20

E

electricity 118
emergencies 118
entry formalities 113–14
Eptapyrgio 74
etiquette and dress 117–18

F

festivals and events 44, 91, 106–8
Fishing Museum 17
Folk Museum of Macedonia and
    Thrace 74
food and drink 83–4, 94–9, 100–101,
    102, 120 see also individual
    locations

G

Glarocavos 35
golf 104
Grigoriou (Mount Athos) 81

H

Hanioti 26–33
healthcare 113, 118, 120–21
horse riding 105

I

Ierissos 63, 65
Ierissos Culture Centre 69
Internet 116

K

Kallithea 20–23, 110
Kanistro 37, 40
Karidi 51
Kastamonitou (Mount Athos) 80
Kastro 91
Kelyfos 59
Kriopigi 24–5

L

Ladadika 73, 77–8
Lake Volvi 104
Litochoro 87
Loutra Spa 37, 40, 105

M

markets 100–101
media 122
Modiano 100
monasteries 9, 63, 66, 79–81
money 114, 121–2, 124
Moni Evangelistrias (Skopelos) 91

motorbikes and scooters 66, 119–20
Mount Athos 9, 51, 63, 65, 79–81
Mount Itamos 56, 58–9
Mount Olympus and Dion 86–8
mountain biking 45, 105
Museum of Byzantine Culture 76
museums and galleries 17, 44, 58, 69, 74, 76, 83, 86, 91, 123

N

Naoussa and Vergina 82–5
national park 86
nature reserve 47
Nea Moudania 15–19
Nea Potidea 15
Nea Roda 65
Nea Skioni 40–41
Neos Marmaras and Porto Carras 58–61, 104, 111
nightlife 20, 26, 33, 39, 50, 54

O

opening times 94–5, 100–101, 110, 122–3
O Pyrgos tis Ouranoupolis 66
Ouranoupolis 63–70, 110

P

Pantokrator (Skiathos) 91
Papadiamantis Museum 91
Paradisos 58
Parthenonas 58
Pefkohori 34–9
Perea 77
Petralona Caves 17
Porto Koufo 56–7
Possidi 40
post 116
Potidea Canal 17–18
Pounta 59
public transport 113, 116, 120

R

religion 106–7, 123
River Axios 104
Rotunda (Thessaloniki) 76
Roussiko (Mount Athos) 80–81

S

safety 87, 102, 103, 120, 121
St Paul's Tower 18
Sani 42–50, 102, 104–5, 110–11
Sarti 54–5
shopping 100–101, 103
Simonos Petras (Mount Athos) 81
Skala Fourkas 40
Skiathos and Skopelos 89–92
snorkelling 22, 28
Spalathronisia islets 59
State Museum of Contemporary Art 76
swimming 51

T

telephones 116, 117
tennis 45, 105
Thessaloniki 8, 72–8, 100–101, 111, 116, 122–3
Thessaloniki Archaeological Museum 76
time differences 124
toilets 124
Tombs of Vergina 83
Toroni 56
Tripiti 63

V

Vlali 100
Vourvourou 51, 53, 102, 111

W

walking and climbing 47, 56, 58–9, 87
watersports 22, 24–5, 28, 47, 54, 103, 105
White Tower (Thessaloniki) 77

X

Xenofontos (Mount Athos) 80
Xina 35

Z

Zografou (Mount Athos) 80
Zygou Monastery 66

ACKNOWLEDGEMENTS

We would like to thank all the photographers, picture libraries and organisations for the loan of the photographs reproduced in this book, to whom copyright in the photograph belongs:
www.sargasso-travelimages.com 9, 16, 19, 25, 27, 29, 31, 36, 46, 48, 53, 55, 57, 64, 67, 68, 71, 75, 90, 93, 95, 101, 109, 115; Dreamstime.com 5 (Natascha Riha), 10–11, (Nikos Pavlakis), 13 (Serbari Enache), 38 (Pavel Savchenkov); Nic Croad/www.go2halkidiki.net 23, 32, 34, 41; Getty Images 84, 106; Photoshot/World Pictures 21, 60; Pictures Colour Library 88; Sani Resort & Oceania Club 103; Wikimedia Commons 59, 79, 104.

Project editor: Rosalind Munro
Layout: Paul Queripel
Proofreaders: Caroline Hunt & Kelly Walker
Indexer: Karolin Thomas

Send your thoughts to
books@thomascook.com

- Found a beach bar, peaceful stretch of sand or must-see sight that we don't feature?

- Like to tip us off about any information that needs a little updating?

- Want to tell us what you love about this handy, little guidebook and, more importantly, how we can make it even handier?

Then here's your chance to tell all! Send us ideas, discoveries and recommendations today and then look out for your valuable input in the next edition of this title.

Email to the above address or write to:
pocket guides Series Editor, Thomas Cook Publishing, PO Box 227, Unit 9, Coningsby Road, Peterborough PE3 8SB, UK.

Useful phrases

English	Greek	Approx pronunciation
BASICS		
Yes	Ναι	*Ne*
No	Οχι	***O*-khee**
Please	Παρακαλώ	*Pa-ra-ka-lh*
Thank you	Ευχαριστώ	*Ef-ha-ri-**sto***
Hello	Γεια σας	*Ya sas*
Goodbye	Αντίο	*An**dee**o*
Excuse me	Με συγχωρείτε	*Me si-nho-**ri**-te*
Sorry	Συγγνώμη	*Sig-**no**-mi*
That's okay	Εντάξει	*En-**ta**-xi*
I don't speak Greek	Δεν μιλώ Ελληνικά	*Den Mi-**lo** (E-li-ni-**ka**)*
Do you speak English?	Μιλάτε Αγγλικά;	*Mi-**la**-te an-gli-**ka**?*
Good morning	Καλημέρα	*Ka-li-**me**-ra*
Good afternoon	χαίρετε	***He**-re-te*
Good evening	Καλησπέρα	*Ka-li-**spe**-ra*
Goodnight	Καληνύχτα	*Ka-li-**nih**-ta*
My name is ...	Ονομάζομαι	*O-no-**ma**-zo-me*
NUMBERS		
One	Ένα	***E**-na*
Two	Δύο	***Di**-o*
Three	Τρία	***Tri**-a*
Four	Τέσσερα	***Te**-se-ra*
Five	Πέντε	***Pen**-te*
Six	Έξι	***E**-xi*
Seven	Επτά	*Ep-**ta***
Eight	Οκτώ	*Ok-**to***
Nine	Εννέα	*E-**ne**-a*
Ten	Δέκα	***De**-ka*
Twenty	Είκοσι	***I**-ko-si*
Fifty	Πενήντα	*Pe-**nin**-ta*
One hundred	Εκατό	*E-ka-to*
SIGNS & NOTICES		
Airport	Αεροδρόμιο	*A-e-rodromio*
Railway station	Σιδηροδρομικός εταμσς	*Sidirodromikos Stathmos*
Smoking/ non-smoking	Για Καπνιστές/ Για μη καπνιστές	*Ya kapnistes/ Ya mikapnistes*
Toilets	Τουαλέτα	*Tualeta*
Ladies/Gentlemen	Γυναικών/Ανδρών	*Yinekon/Andron*